PIRATES

The True and Surprising
Story of the Pirates of the
Caribbean & Blackbeard The
Pirate Terror of the Sea

Patrick Auerbach

CONTENTS

Disclaimer Notice:

Please note the information contained within this document is for educational and entertainment purposes only. Every attempt has been made to provide accurate, up-to-date, and reliable complete information. No warranties of any kind are expressed or implied. Readers acknowledge that the author is not engaging in the rendering of legal, financial, medical or professional advice.

By reading this document, the reader agrees that under no circumstances are we responsible for any losses, direct or indirect, which are incurred as a result of the use of the information contained within this document, including, but not limited to errors, omissions, or inaccuracies.

INTRODUCTION

There can be very few of us who did not dress up as pirates or play "walking the plank" games in childhood. The image of a swashbuckling, peg-legged sea captain with a skull and crossbones flag on his ship, a parrot on his shoulder, and a patch on his eye is one that has been passed down through many generations, but did such characters ever really exist?

In recent years, the imaginations of young and old alike were sparked once again by the creation of Captain Jack Sparrow in Disney's Pirates of the Caribbean, but do these tales of daring tell us anything about real life in what has become known as the Golden Age of Piracy?

The aim of this book is to tell the tale of real life as a pirate of the Caribbean through the lives (and deaths) of history's most notorious pirate captains... and to sort the facts from the fiction along the way. Did pirates really have parrots, did they all drink rum, did 'X' really mark the spot where they buried their treasure and did they really all say, "Arrrr, me hearties!"?

Read on to discover the answers to these and many more questions about real life as a pirate of the Caribbean.

WHO WERE THE PIRATES OF THE CARIBBEAN?

According to maritime history, the Golden Age of Piracy began in the 1650s and continued to the 1730s, but many historians now believe that the majority of plundering and looting we associate with piracy today took place over just a few short years from around 1716 to 1726. This coincided with the end of the War of the Spanish Succession which meant that fewer European navies occupied the seas in the area and a great many well-trained sailors found themselves out of work as a consequence.

The Treaty of Utrecht ended the War of the Spanish Succession in 1713, but before it was signed Spain and France were at war with England, the Netherlands, and other European nations including Portugal. After the signing, many of the merchant sailors previously employed by their country's government found themselves out of work and the privateers who had taken payment in the form of a portion of the spoils of war were no longer gainfully employed. For this reason, many turned to a life of piracy... after all; the art of plundering was what they knew best.

COMMON TYPES
OF PIRATES:

Buccaneers – the name 'buccaneer' comes from the French 'boucan' which describes the type of meat these men, mainly Frenchmen, used to sell to passing ships before they turned to a life of piracy in around 1650. This 'buccaneering' period continued until around 1680, and towards the end of the 17th century, the term buccaneer became synonymous with a pirate. Buccaneers were skilled raiders on land and they were less inclined to raid at sea, but their attacks were almost exclusively on Spanish coastal towns and ships so they were supported by the English and all other nations at war with Spain. Most buccaneers considered themselves to be privateers, with many carrying letters of marque which served as legal proof that they were sponsored by wealthy individuals and not operating as independent pirates.

Privateers – in a nutshell, privateers were commissioned by the government of their country or wealthy individuals to attack and raid enemy ships in times of war. This meant that privateers were effectively licenced to steal and they carried with them a letter of marque which identified them as 'legal' raiders. However, many wanted more than their 'contracted' share of the spoils and the line between privateer and outright pirate was often crossed. In effect, provided no valuable diplomatic or trading relations were damaged, privateers pretty much did whatever they pleased – and got away with it.

During this period in history there were rich pickings to be had at sea as the number of ships carrying hugely valuable cargoes across open oceans was on the rise. Ships sailed out of Europe carrying weapons and other manufactured goods to the coast of Africa where they were traded for slaves. The slaves were then shipped to the Caribbean where they were traded for tobacco, cocoa, and sugar which was then shipped back to Europe. This was known as the Triangular Transatlantic Slave Trade, but another triangular route involved the shipping of raw materials such as rum and preserved cod to Europe where a portion of it was traded for manufactured goods. These were then shipped to the Caribbean to be traded for molasses and sugar and then shipped to New England. These triangular trading routes created prime targets for pirates operating in Caribbean waters.

In 1715, a group of pirates swooped on Spanish divers attempting to recover the cargo of a galleon that had sunk off the coast of Florida. This would become the richest raid of the Golden Age as the cargo was gold. The pirates were English ex-privateers Henry Jennings, Charles Vane, Samuel Bellamy, Edward England, and Benjamin Hornigold who became known as the Flying Gang – but more on these infamous rogues later... Laden with loot, the group returned to the expected pirate safe haven of Jamaica only to discover the ports of Kingston and Port Royal were closed to them and the governor was refusing to allow them to spend their plundered gold on the island. It was this that prompted the infamous gang to create a new island base in the Bahamas. The island of New Providence had been abandoned since the war. The town of Nassau which had easy access to the busy shipping lanes of the Florida Strait and a harbor that was too shallow for Royal Navy ships to enter became their new 'home', along with many more pirate recruits who joined them.

Part of the settlement after the war was that

English ships could sail into Spain's New World colonies to supply slaves. Many unemployed sailors found work on board these slave ships, but with so many mariners looking for work merchant ship owners were able to get away with paying a pittance in wages and providing very poor work conditions. In fact, the death rate among sailors on these voyages was often higher than among the slaves they were transporting. With more and more ships sailing in and out of the New World and working conditions becoming steadily worse, more and more sailors opted to chance their luck in the altogether freer world of piracy.

Chapter Summary

So, who were the pirates of the Caribbean?

On the whole, they were trained sailors and skilled seamen who found themselves out of work and struggling to make ends meet.

WAS LIFE AS
A PIRATE A
FREER LIFE?

The 'pirate code' is something we all associate with life aboard a pirate ship. Story books and movies create images of a fair and just environment in which all crewmen are equal and all are entitled to a vote on the appointment of their captain, officers, and other such affairs, but was living as a pirate really a freer life than life as a sailor?

The 'pirate code', also known as pirate articles or Articles of Agreement, happened when each captain drew up his own version of the pirate code or rules for his ship. This meant there were as many variations as there were pirate captains but each code included rules on disciplinary procedures, compensation payments for any injuries sustained, and the share of loot each crewmate was entitled to.

To become a pirate crew member, each man had to swear an oath of allegiance and sign the articles. Many couldn't write and therefore had to make their mark on the articles instead, but once signed, they were displayed in a prominent place on the ship for all to see. Swearing allegiance was often done over a Bible but legend has it that when no Bible was available, the oath may have been sworn over an axe, crossed swords, a skull, or even sitting astride the ship's cannon.

Many unemployed sailors willingly 'signed up' as pirate crewmen but many new recruits came from captured ships and were forced into signing the articles when faced with the threat of torture or death if they did not. This was particularly the case for seamen with useful skills such as navigation or carpentry so for these men, life as a pirate was clearly not a freer life. However, compared to privateering articles, the pirate articles did offer a much fairer system of divvying up the loot so each crew member generally received an equal share of any plunder... but this depended on the captain. As each captain drew up his own version of the pirate code for his ship, some chose to draw up different versions for different voyages, thereby changing the 'rules' on the distribution of booty depending on the intended target. With this being the case, reality as a pirate crewman would often be a far cry from the storybook image of equality for all.

THE PIRATE CODE

T here was no standard pirate code, but a few original versions have remained intact through the centuries and they provide an insight into the typical content of early 18th-century pirate articles. In the majority of cases, pirate articles were burned or thrown overboard by the captain and crew if the ship was about to be captured as any such paperwork would be used against them when facing trial. It's known that crewmen were more likely to escape execution if they had not signed the articles and for this reason, some recruits would ask to be forced, albeit in a pretend manner so that they could claim they'd signed against their will if captured.

Captain Charles Johnson's book, A General History of the Robberies and Murders of the Most Notorious Pirates, published in Britain in 1724 contains most of the surviving information on authentic pirate articles, although it's accepted that not every aspect of the book is entirely factual. No one knows the true identity of the author but it's popularly believed that Charles Johnson was a pseudonym for Daniel Defoe, author of Robinson Crusoe, or perhaps Nathaniel Mist who was a British journalist and experienced sailor. Some believe that the author may even have been a pirate himself as many of the detailed biographies and accounts of notorious pirates contained within the book's pages have since been verified by research.

THE ARTICLES OF CAPTAIN JOHN PHILLIPS

In 1724, pirate crewmen joining Captain John Phillips on board the ship Revenge signed the following articles:

Article I. Every Man Shall obey civil Command; the Captain shall have one full Share and a half of all Prizes; the Master, Carpenter, Boatswain, and Gunner shall have one Share and quarter.

Article II. If any Man shall offer to run away, or keep any Secret from the Company, he shall be marooned with one Bottle of Powder, one Bottle of Water, one small Arm, and Shot.

Article III. If any Man shall steal any Thing in the Company, or game, to the Value of a Piece of Eight, he shall be marooned or shot.

Article IV. If any time we shall meet another Marooner that Man shall sign his Articles without the Consent of our Company shall suffer such Punishment as the Captain and Company shall think fit.

Article V. That Man that shall strike another whilst these Articles are in force, shall receive Moses' Law (that is, 40 Stripes lacking one) on the bare Back.

Article VI. That Man that shall snap his Arms, or smoke Tobacco in the Hold, without a Cap to his Pipe, or carry a Candle lighted without a Lanthorn, shall suffer the same Punishment as in the former Article.

Article VII. That Man that shall not keep his Arms clean, fit for an Engagement, or neglect his Business, shall be cut off from his Share, and suffer such other Punishment as the Captain and the Company shall think fit.

Article VIII. If any Man shall lose a Joint in time of an Engagement, shall have 400 Pieces of Eight; if a Limb, 800.

Article IX. If at any time you meet with a prudent Woman, that Man that offers to meddle with her, without her Consent, shall suffer present Death.

Other surviving articles include those of Captains Edward Low and George Lowther drawn up in 1722, John Gow found on board his ship in 1729, and those believed to have been drawn up by Henry Morgan in the late 1600s.

Notable Articles Include

• That every man shall keep his watch night and day, and at the hour of eight in the evening every one shall retire from gaming and drinking in order to attend his respective station.

• He that sees a Sail first, shall have the best Pistol or Small Arm aboard of her.

• That no man shall open, or declare to any person or persons, who they are, or what designs they are upon; and any persons so offending shall be punished with immediate death.

• That no man shall give, or dispose of, the ship's provisions; but everyone shall have an equal share.

• If any Gold, Jewels, Silver, &c. be found on Board of any Prize or Prizes to the value of a Piece of Eight, & the finder does not deliver it to the Quarter Master in the space of 24 hours he shall suffer what Punishment the Captain and the Majority of the Company shall think fit.

• He that shall be found Guilty of Cowardice in the time of engagements, shall suffer what Punishment the Captain and the Majority of the Company shall think fit.

- The fund of all payments under the articles is the stock of what is gotten by the expedition, following the same law as other pirates, that is, No prey, No pay.

- And, according to Captain Charles Johnson: Every man to be called fairly in turn, by list, on board of prizes because, (over and above their proper share) they were on these occasions allowed a shift of clothes: but if they defrauded the company to the value of a dollar in plate, jewels, or money, marooning was their punishment. If the robbery was only betwixt one another, they contented themselves with slitting the ears and nose of him that was guilty, and set him on shore, not in an uninhabited place, but somewhere, where he was sure to encounter hardships.

Each pirate captain created his own version of the code for his ship, but the need to have a pirate code in the first place came from personal experiences of working under harsh commanders on board naval or merchant ships and a desire to create a better life for themselves and their crewmen. The ultimate desire was, of course, to become rich quickly and live a life of leisure but the most successful pirate captains knew that creating a fairer and better life for their crewmen was the quickest and most effective way to generate a better life for themselves.

It can be argued that willing pirate recruits were violent, lawless men who chose to rebel against society and the restraints placed upon them by the tyrant rulers of the day. However, signing the articles gave pirate crewmen a vote on matters that affected their lives including who should be given the role of captain, so the 'pirate society' this created was effectively ahead of its time in terms of establishing a democratic society.

Chapter Summary

Was life as a pirate a freer life?

In terms of equality, compensation and fair payment, life as a pirate was a freer and better life for many crewmen. However, the Captain and Quartermaster still ruled so the reality on many ships was that the rules changed as often as the wind. If the Captain took a dislike to you, you were gone.

WHO WAS
THE MOST
SUCCESSFUL
PIRATE?

I t's fair to say that Edward Teach (or Thatch), better known as Blackbeard, is perhaps the most famous pirate of the Golden Age of Piracy. But was he the most successful? Well, the short answer is no, but more on Blackbeard's story later. The title of most successful pirate goes to a captain who became at least five times richer than Blackbeard. His name was Bartholomew Roberts... otherwise known as Black Bart.

BLACK BART

Born in Wales in 1682, Bartholomew Roberts first went to sea at the age of 13 on board a merchant ship. By 1719 he was the third mate on the Princess, a slave ship. When the Princess was later captured by pirate Captain Howell Davis and his pirate crew, Bartholomew Roberts was forced to join them as his skills as a navigator made him an extremely useful acquisition. He soon came around to the idea of being a pirate and he's quoted to have said:
"In an honest service there is thin commons, low wages, and hard labor; in this, plenty and satiety, pleasure and ease, liberty, and power; and who would not balance creditor on this side, when all the hazard that is run for it, at worst, is only a sour look or two at choking. No, a merry life and a short one, shall be my motto."

Only six weeks after his capture, Bartholomew Roberts became Captain of Howell Davis' pirate fleet. Davis was killed on the island of Principe off the west coast of Africa where he'd sailed freely into the harbor by raising the colors of a British man o' war – a powerful Royal Navy warship. He had intended to lure the governor of the island onto his ship and then capture him so he could be held to ransom. However, the governor invited Davis to join him for a drink at the fort before boarding the ship, all the while arranging for his men to ambush and kill him on the way.

A vote was held among the remaining crewmen to elect a new captain; Bartholomew Roberts won. His first mission as captain was to avenge the death of Davis and he led an attack on Principe in which a great many islanders died, and everything that could be stolen was taken back to the ship. From this point forwards, 'Black Bart's' reputation as a "pistol-proof", brave, and intelligent individual grew and he and his crew went on to successfully capture over 400 ships, acquiring loot with an estimated value of around £23 million.

In one raid, Black Bart and his pirate crew made off with a diamond-encrusted cross on its way to the King of Portugal along with around 40,000 gold moidores (Portuguese gold coins). However, after another successful raid, one captain in his pirate fleet sailed off with more than his fair share of the loot and this prompted Black Bart to create a set of rules that became known as The Pirate Code.

Black Bart's first defeat came in 1720. The people of Barbados and Martinique had joined forces to target all of the pirate ships in Black Bart's fleet and they were sending out their own ships to hunt him down. In one attack, the ship Black Bart was captaining was hit hard and he was forced to retreat to avoid sinking. He headed for Dominica where he would be able to make repairs, but 20 injured crewmen died on the journey. This was a blow that led Black Bart to swear he'd get his revenge on his attackers.

His opportunity to avenge the attack came after sailing north in the direction of Newfoundland where he terrorized the area by raiding ports, setting fire to docked ships, and at one point capturing 15 ships in just three days. On one raid, he approached a man o' war by flying the colors of a French merchant ship and claiming to have information on the whereabouts of Black Bart. He and his crew then captured the ship and to his surprise, he discovered the governor of Martinique was on board. Black Bart had the governor hanged there and then in revenge.

In 1721 after setting sail for Africa, one of the best captains in Black Bart's pirate fleet turned tail and headed back to the Caribbean in the dead of night. With one ship lost, Black Bart then had to abandon his own ship when it became too leaky. However, he had recently joined forces with Montigny la Palisse, a French pirate, so they used his ship to continue on their way. Despite the loss of two ships from his fleet, Black Bart still managed to capture two French ships after they attacked near Guinea.

Sailing towards Sierra Leone, Black Bart discovered that the seas in the area were undefended as HMS Swallow and HMS Weymouth, both heavily armored British warships, had sailed from the area and would not be returning for several months. The pirate fleet took full advantage of the situation, capturing merchant ships and taking control of Quidah harbor, and they continued to dominate until the return of the British warships the following year.

BLACK BART'S DEMISE

In 1722, HMS Swallow spotted Black Bart's fleet in Cape Lopez. Most of the pirate crewmen were drunk as they were celebrating the successful capture of another ship, making it easy for the warship to approach unnoticed. When the alarm was finally raised, Black Bart attempted to escape the Swallow's devastating broadside cannon attacks by sailing quickly past her and out of the harbor, but his attempt failed as his navigator made a couple of crucial mistakes that left them a sitting duck in the Swallow's firing line. The first round of cannon fire killed Black Bart instantly.

Black Bart's body was buried at sea by his crew before they surrendered so that it would not be used as a public example of the perils of piracy, but most of the crew were then tried and hung.

The captain of HMS Swallow was knighted for ending Black Bart's reign of terror on the seas and many historians believe the death of Black Bart effectively ended the Golden Age of Piracy as it began a trend of expanding the reach of law-enforcing naval ships into previously lawless open seas.

Chapter Summary

So, who was the most successful pirate?

In terms of captured ships and accumulated loot, Black Bart is arguably the most successful pirate of the Golden Age of Piracy. However, his success and the success of many other pirates may have been inspired by Captain Henry Every, a notorious pirate on the first 'Pirate Round' in the Indian Ocean.

WHO WAS HENRY EVERY?

The Pirate Round is a term used to describe a piracy route in the Indian Ocean around the end of the 17th century. Thomas Tew, also known as the Rhode Island Pirate, coined the term after successfully raiding ships off the Cape of Good Hope. His success inspired others, including Henry Every, to operate as pirates in the same area.

After Tew's first successful raid, he joined forces with Every and others to target a ship owned by the Mughal Empire in India. Tew was killed in the raid but Every successfully plundered riches worth at least £325,000. The Emperor of the Mughal Empire was outraged by the attack and the damage to trade caused by Every's actions. This led to the British East India Company putting a bounty on his head and appointing William Kidd as a privateer to hunt him down along with Thomas Kew and every other pirate on the Pirate Round. At the time of his appointment, it was unknown that Thomas Tew had already been killed and that Henry Every would never be found.

EARLY CAREER

After the raid, Henry Every vanished and nothing is known of his whereabouts after 1696. In fact, very little is known about the rest of Henry Every's life. It's known that he was born in England in 1659 and began his seafaring career working aboard a British naval ship, HMS Rubert. He was discharged from the Royal Navy in 1690 and took employment on board a slave trading ship in Africa. It's believed that Every ran an illegal but highly lucrative slave trading operation between 1690 and 1692 before becoming the first mate on a Spanish warship named Charles II. After promises made to the crew were not fulfilled, Every headed a mutiny and took control of the ship, renaming her the Fancy.

In 1695, several successful raids later, Every and his crew sailed the Fancy to the Straits of Bab-el-Mandeb to meet with Thomas Tew and several other pirate ships in preparation for the attack on the Mughal Empire trading ship. Captain Tew had

60 crewmen on board his ship the Amity; Captain Joseph Faro joined them with another 60 crewmen on board the Portsmouth Adventure. Richard Want was captain of the Dolphin and he had a further 60 crewmen, Thomas Wake captained the Susanna with 70 crewmen and William Mayes had a crew of around 40 on his ship, the Pearl.

After pursuing the Mughal ship the Ganj-i-Sawai for several days, the pirate ships finally captured her escort ship, the Fateh Muhammed. The Dolphin had fallen behind on the way so the crew had switched to the Fancy and the Dolphin was burned. The Susanna had also fallen back but she managed to catch up with the others as they began to overtake the Mughal convoy. Every the crewmen on board the Fancy captured the Fateh Muhammad and plundered a haul of around £50,000, but with so many pirates taking a share, each man received only a small portion of the treasure.

It took several more days to catch up with the Ganj-i-Sawai and the Amity was no longer with them as Thomas Tew had been killed in his attempt to capture the Fateh Muhammad. It was now the Fancy, the Portsmouth Adventure and the Pearl against the heavily armed Mughal ship. The Ganj-i-Sawai, which in translation means "Exceeding Treasure", had 62 guns and over 400 guards armed with muskets but an explosion caused by one of her cannons killed a number of the gunners and the confusion gave Every the opportunity to damage her mainmast with a broadside shot.

PIRATE CRUELTY

O n boarding the ship, the pirates rampaged along every deck and terrorized the 600 passengers, torturing them to discover the whereabouts of hidden loot and raping the women in retaliation for the death of pirate crewmen. The huge haul of treasure taken included 500,000 pieces of gold and silver, making it one of the most lucrative raids in the history of piracy alongside the Spanish galleon raid carried out by the Flying Gang two decades later.

It's believed that the surviving captains headed for the French island of Réunion where each crew member received a £1000 share of the loot along with a handful of gemstones, more than any man expected to earn in a lifetime. After a short time spent in the Bahamas in the pirate haven of New Providence, the exact whereabouts of Henry Every become unclear. Legend has it that he established a pirate utopia on a tropical island that has never been identified and lived out the rest of his days as the King of Pirates in Libertalia. However, others believe he returned to England where he was duped out of his riches while attempting to sell his treasures and died a penniless beggar.

HENRY EVERY'S LEGACY

T he truth may never be known but Henry Every captured the imagination of a generation and his exploits turned him into a folk hero. Black Bart and other infamous pirates of the early 18th century were children at the time of Every's raid on the Mughal treasure ship and tales of his daring and mysterious disappearance undoubtedly inspired many of the next generation of pirates.

Edward England, one of the infamous Flying Gang, spent most of his pirating career raiding Mughal ships in the Indian Ocean just as Every had done some 20 years before him. After capturing a slave ship off the coast of Africa in 1720 and renaming it Fancy, England then found himself marooned on Mauritius by his crew after denying them permission to torture those they'd captured. He floated on a makeshift raft to an island off of Mauritius that many believed to be Every's Libertalia, but this was not the reality he found. England ended his days as an alcoholic and a beggar, although many authors of pirate biographies have since described Edward England as the pirate who perhaps came closest to living out the Henry Every legend in his brief yet spectacular career.

Chapter Summary

Who was Henry Avery?

Henry Avery vanished in 1696 after pulling off one of the richest raids in the history of piracy. His exploits became legendary and the fact that he evaded capture despite a hefty bounty on his head no doubt inspired many down-trodden seamen to chance their luck aboard a pirate ship in the Golden Age of Piracy.

The hunt for Every lasted 10 years, but he was never found.

WHAT BECAME OF WILLIAM KIDD?

Having been commissioned to hunt down Henry Every and others like him in 1695, privateer William Kidd turned to a life of piracy himself.

In 1689, Englishman William Kidd was part of a privateer crew in the Caribbean. After successfully commandeering a French ship, he was appointed captain of the ship which was renamed Blessed William in honor of King William III. As a privateer, he was to protect the island of Nevis (a British colony at the time) from French attackers, and in return he was to keep the spoils of war as payment for his services. In effect, he was licensed to steal.

The Blessed William joined a Royal Navy fleet

in an attack on a French sugar plantation. The town of Marie Galante was raided and William Kidd secured around £2000 in loot. He was then ordered to join another Royal Navy fleet on a mission to attack French warships at sea. Kidd's crew refused as they were only paid in shares of plundered loot, something they would not find on warships. Led by Robert Culliford, the crew stole the Blessed William and all of Captain Kidd's stored loot when he was ashore one evening. Kidd was given another ship, the Antigua.

PIRATE HUNTER

I n 1695, William Kidd was appointed as a privateer to rid the Indian ocean of Henry Every and other pirates like him, including Robert Culliford who had stolen the Blessed William. It was rumored that Culliford was sailing with a surgeon named Jon Death and that they were attacking ships by firing china dishes from their cannons to shred the sails. However, as Kidd was funded by four wealthy noblemen, there can be little doubt that they expected him to take advantage of any opportunity to raid enemy ships so that their investment would be recouped with a healthy share of all booty taken. The King issued Captain Kidd with written permission to apprehend all pirates of any nationality and granted him special permission to attack and plunder all French ships. However, it was also made clear in writing that he must not attack any ship that was a friend of the Crown: "We do strictly charge and command you, as you will answer to the contrary at your peril, that you do not, in any manner, offend or molest our friends or allies, their ships or subjects, by color or pretense of these presents, or the authority granted."

William Kidd and his crew set sail from New York in 1696 aboard the Adventure Galley and headed for the Indian Ocean. In 1697, he had yet to capture any ships or plunder any booty and under pressure from a disgruntled crew, he turned to piracy. Some success was had with raids on a number of smaller ships but after a failed attack on a ship carrying coffee from Yemen, his crew wanted to target a Dutch ship in the area. Kidd refused and this almost led to mutiny. In a heated argument, Kidd struck his gunner William Moore on the head with a metal-ringed bucket and Moore died soon after from his injuries.

In 1698, Kidd captured the Quedagh Merchant, a treasure-laden Armenian ship with a cargo of sugar, silk, muslins, calico, opium, saltpeter, and iron that had a value of around £70,000. The Adventure Galley had become leaky so Kidd abandoned her and kept the Quedagh Merchant, renaming her Adventure Prize, and set sail for the West Indies with his booty.

A WANTED MAN

On arrival in Anguilla, Kidd discovered he was being accused of piracy and was a wanted man. Two years had passed since his voyage had begun and attitudes toward piracy had now changed. England no longer turned a blind eye to privateering activities and all acts of piracy were now deemed criminal acts. All along the coast of the American colonies ships were on the hunt for pirates, so Kidd abandoned the Adventure Prize and bought a new ship, the Antonio, before sailing to New York to plead his innocence.

Captain Kidd negotiated a pardon from the English authorities after pleading that his crew had forced him into acts of piracy. He set sail for Boston but stopped on the way to bury some of his plundered loot on Gardeners Island and Block Island. The governor of New England, one of the original investors in Kidd's voyage, had him arrested in Boston and he was sent to England in

1700 to be put on trial. In what we now know to be a shamelessly flawed and rigged trial procedure, William Kidd was found guilty of the murder of William Moore and several acts of piracy; he was hanged in 1701.

It took two attempts to hang Captain Kidd as the first rope placed around his neck broke and he dropped to the ground still alive. Once dead, his body was chained to a post and left there until three tides had washed over it. His corpse was then tarred and placed in an iron cage, known as a gibbet, and displayed for all to see at the mouth of the River Thames. This ritual was intended to serve as a warning to any other seamen considering a life of piracy.

Many believe William Kidd was the victim of an unfair justice system and the rich individuals who funded his voyage lost none of their wealth and remained in positions of power. Kidd had made several desperate attempts to save himself by promising to reveal the whereabouts of his buried booty, and after his death, the legend of buried pirate treasure grew. To this day, treasure hunters are still searching for Kidd's loot. Some was found on Gardeners Island but whether or not any other treasure actually exists remains a mystery.

Chapter Summary

So, what became of William Kidd?

Captain William Kidd went down in history as the pirate hunter who turned pirate... and paid for it with his life after a questionable trial.

After his death, his legend grew, and the belief that pirates buried their treasure gathered strength- fuelled to this day by tales such as *Treasure Island.*

WHO IS THE MOST FAMOUS PIRATE OF THEM ALL?

I t could be argued that in today's world, Jack Sparrow is the most famous pirate of them all – but he's a fictional character. Blackbeard, on the other hand, is not only a very famous pirate name but a very real pirate.

Blackbeard is thought to have been born in England as Edward Teach or Thatch. Little is known of his early life but it's believed that he may have developed his skills as a sailor working aboard privateering ships around the time of Queen Anne's War, the name given to the elements of the War of the Spanish Succession taking place in the British colonies. It's known that he joined

Captain Benjamin Hornigold, of Flying Gang fame, on the island of New Providence around 1716. He was given command of a sloop captured by Hornigold and the pair set about capturing and raiding many more ships in the area liberating at least 100 barrels of wine along the way, and in one raid taking only the Madeira wine and leaving the rest of the ship's cargo on board as they scuttled her. In 1717, the former military officer turned pirate Stede Bonnet joined them. With his ship the Revenge and a crew of around 70 men they became a formidable pirate fleet. Bonnet's men were unhappy with his leadership so Teach took over command of the Revenge – whether or not this was done with Bonnet's permission is unclear. Soon after this, they captured a large French slave ship, La Concorde, which Teach renamed Queen Anne's Revenge. The crew of La Concorde was given Teach's smallest sloop which they promptly renamed Mauvaise Rencontre, meaning "bad meeting".

Toward the end of 1717, Hornigold retired from piracy after being demoted by his crew. As a British privateer, Hornigold had only ever attacked enemy ships and this was a policy he'd carried over into his acts of piracy. However, his crew soon found it unbearable to watch British ships laden with valuable cargo go sailing by untouched and they took the matter into their own hands. Hornigold took the Ranger and a sloop they'd captured with him. In 1718, he accepted the King's Pardon from the newly appointed Captain General and Governor in Chief in the Bahamas, Woodes Rogers.

TEACH BECOMES BLACKBEARD

Edward Teach continued to terrorize the seas and his fearsome appearance led to him becoming known as Blackbeard. His beard grew bushy and long and he's believed to have braided it with black ribbons, tying gunpowder-laced ropes into the braids and lighting them as he stormed a ship. Already a man of considerable size, he made himself larger than life by wearing a crimson red coat, long boots, and a wide hat, under which he would wear more burning ropes fastened into his hair. Around his waist, he carried two swords and across his chest, he displayed a collection of pistols and knives kept ready for action in ribbon sashes. In Charles Johnson's book, A General History of Pirates, Blackbeard is described as "such a figure that imagination cannot form an idea of a fury from hell to look more frightful."

Whether or not the image of Blackbeard created by writers in the 18th century is a true reflection of his appearance or an embellishment designed to attract more readers may never be known, but his reputation alone was enough to make most merchant ships surrender without putting up any sort of fight... often at the mere sight of his flag. It was a common ploy of Blackbeard's to appear friendly by raising the national flag of the ships he targeted on his own mast. This would allow him to draw near, waiting until the very last moment to hoist his pirate flag.

RUTHLESS REPUTATION

His appearance and reputation struck fear into the hearts of all who encountered him but if a ship chose not to surrender, Blackbeard's crew struck hard - usually targeting the crewman at the ship's wheel first and foremost so that it would be left drifting. Grappling hooks were then used to pull the ship near and Blackbeard and his pirate crew would leap aboard... the crew of the 40-gun Queen Anne's Revenge had now grown to as many as 250 men.

Once a ship was captured, all of her crew and passengers would be taken hostage while the cabins were stripped of any jewelry, gold, silver, and coins that could be found. Blackbeard was cunning, fearless, and ruthless but despite his reputation for cruel treatment, no written or verified record exists of him ever murdering or harming any of his captives. However, there are many legendary tales surrounding his behavior.

Tales Of Blackbeard

• According to one tale, Blackbeard once dealt with a passenger who refused to part with his diamond ring by simply chopping off his whole finger.

• In another, it's claimed that Blackbeard shot and killed his own first mate, then said to his crewmen, "If I don't shoot one or two of you now and then, you'll forget who I am."

• And, according to Captain Charles Johnson's book, after drinking his fill of rum on one occasion, Blackbeard went with his crew into the ship's hold, saying "Come, let us make a hell of our own, and try how long we can bear it." The hatches were then closed and a number of pots were filled with brimstone and set alight. It didn't take long for the men to begin coughing and spluttering as the sulfurous fumes filled the air. They made a break for fresh air, but Blackbeard stayed in the hold. When he eventually emerged, he bellowed, "Damn ye, ye yellow (curse word)! I'm a better man than all ye milksops put together."

• But, perhaps most frighteningly of all, it was said that

Blackbeard was so strong that he could slice a man from his head to his waist with just one blow of his cutlass.

BLACKBEARD'S DEMISE

Blackbeard lived in the pirate haven of Nassau where he was a magistrate of the "Privateers Republic". He had bases in the Bahamas and the Carolinas, and in his most famous raid, he gathered a small flotilla of pirate ships and blockaded Charleston port in South Carolina where he plundered five merchant ships. The passengers on one of the captured ships were held hostage by Blackbeard and he demanded a ransom of one chest of medicines. For some reason, the Charleston residents were slow in delivering the ransom and Blackbeard appeared quite prepared to murder every one of the hostages; women and children included. When the chest of medicines finally appeared some days later, the hostages were released unharmed, but also without their clothes.

Blackbeard and his pirate fleet then sailed to North Carolina where he grounded the Queen Anne's Revenge on a sand bank. It's believed that this may have been a deliberate act and many of his crew accused him of attempting to increase his own share of the loot by downsizing his fleet and therefore the size of his crew. Most of his crewmen were beached or marooned and Blackbeard sailed off in his sloop, the Adventure, after stripping the other ships of their treasure.

Unlike Henry Every, Blackbeard did not welcome the arrival of Royal Governor Woodes Rogers in Nassau or the King's Pardons he offered to all pirates living there. He chose to settle in North Carolina where he gained unofficial protection from Governor Charles Eden, who apparently accepted booty from Blackbeard in return. Blackbeard eventually accepted an official pardon from Eden, but his 'retirement' from pirating didn't last long and his return to the seas attracted the attention of the Governor of Virginia, Alexander Spotswood.

ROBERT
MAYNARD

Blackbeard was out of Spotswood's jurisdiction but the governor didn't like the fact that such a ferocious and notorious character lived nearby. He decided to rid the area of Blackbeard once and for all and arranged for a party of experienced sailors to hunt him down. Blackbeard tended to operate in waters that were too shallow for most navy ships to maneuver in easily so Spotswood hired two smaller sloops and put them under the command of Lieutenant Robert Maynard. The Lieutenant was offered a reward of £100, and the crew- 30 sailors from HMS Pearl and 25 from HMS Lyme - slightly less in rewards, but only if they were successful in finishing Blackbeard off for good. The sloops, the Ranger, and Jane, set sail from James River on November 11th, 1718.

On the evening of November 21st, Maynard and his sloops found Blackbeard's sloop anchored off the North Carolina coastline near Ocracoke Island. He made the decision to wait until the following morning's more favorable tides before attacking. A small boat sent out at dawn on November 22nd was quickly fired upon; Blackbeard had spent the night waiting for Maynard to make a move. Blackbeard then cut his anchor and made a break for a narrow channel, but Maynard was in hot pursuit. Both of Maynard's sloops then ran aground and he and Blackbeard were close enough to exchange heated words. There are several written accounts of the dialogue, with Maynard's version as follows: "At our first salutation, he drank Damnation to me and my Men, whom he stil'd Cowardly Puppies, saying, He would neither give nor take Quarter."

Maynard's sloops eventually floated free but there was no wind for sails so the crews rowed towards Blackbeard. Jane was hit hard with a surprise broadside attack; seven crewmen were killed and 10 others wounded forcing Maynard and the Ranger to continue the attack with just one sloop. He managed to cause enough damage to Blackbeard's sloop to force her ashore, then ordered a good proportion of his crew to go below decks into the hold. Blackbeard now had a pirate crew of just 19 men, and on seeing the decks of the Ranger mainly empty as she approached, he jumped aboard with only 10 men.

Maynard's hidden crew sprang from below decks and a fierce hand-to-hand battle began. The '**Boston News-Letter**' printed the following account of the event:

> "Maynard and Teach themselves begun the fight with their swords, Maynard making a thrust, the point of his sword against Teach's cartridge box, bent it to the hilt. Teach broke the guard of it, and wounded Maynard's fingers but did not disable him, whereupon he jumped back and threw away his sword and fired his pistol which wounded Teach. Demelt struck in between them with his sword and cut Teach's face pretty much; in the interim both companies engaged in Maynard's sloop. Later during the battle, while Teach was loading his pistol he finally died from blood loss. Maynard then cut off his head and hung it from his bow."

It's popularly reported that Blackbeard had over 20 stab wounds and five gunshot wounds before he died. After his decapitation, his remains were thrown overboard by his crew, and legend has it that the headless body swam several times around the Adventure in search of its head before the sloop finally sank.

Maynard returned home with Blackbeard's head to claim his £100 reward. The head was later placed on a spike in Bath Town, North Carolina, and all but two of Blackbeard's surviving crewmen were hung and their corpses displayed in gibbets.

Chapter Summary

Who is the most famous pirate of them all?

From 1716 to 1718, Blackbeard became the most feared pirate in the Caribbean and on the Atlantic. His reign of terror lasted just two years but his legacy lives on to this day, with his fearsome image continuing to inspire the creation of many pirate characters in books and films. In 1996, the sunken remains of a ship believed to be Blackbeard's *Queen Anne's Revenge* were discovered off the coast of North Carolina and thousands of tourists now visit each year.

Some 300 years after his death, Blackbeard's fame has yet to fade.

WERE ALL PIRATES MEN?

It's commonly believed that all pirates were men- in fact, it's often told that pirates believed it to be bad luck if a woman sailed aboard a pirate ship. However, two female pirates were known to be active in the Golden Age of Piracy and both sailed with Captain John Rackham, better known as Calico Jack. Their names were Anne Bonny and Mary Read.

CALICO JACK

J ohn Rackham was born in England in the latter years of the 17th century. As with other pirates of this period, very little is known of his early life and this is in part due to pirates often using aliases in order to protect their family name. However, it's known that Rackham was serving as quartermaster under pirate Captain Charles Vane, one of the famed Flying Gang, in the early part of 1718 and living in the 'pirate home' of Nassau on the island of New Providence.

When Governor Woodes Rogers arrived on the island in the summer of 1718 to offer King's Pardons to all of the pirates based there, Vane and Rackham were among the die-hard pirates who refused and chose to carry on with their pirating ways. Later that year, Vane and a pirate crew of 90 men, including Rackham, encountered a heavily-armed French warship. Rackham and the majority of the crew were keen to fight but Vane opted to make a run for it and avoid a battle. Shortly after, the crew ousted Vane from his command position and voted Rackham in as captain. Vane and the 15 or so crewmen who'd backed him were then marooned.

Before the year was out, Rackham and his crew had captured the Kingston, a merchant ship with rich cargo. However, the raid took place within sight of outraged merchants in Port Royal who immediately sent out bounty hunters to track them down. Early the following year, the hunters found Rackham's ship anchored off Cuba. Rackham and the majority of his crew had gone ashore and hidden in woods to escape capture. However, they could only watch as their ship and all of her treasures were taken away.

Rackham, who became known as Calico Jack due to his taste for brightly-colored Indian Calico cloth clothing, had little impact as a pirate in the Caribbean compared to the likes of Black Bart and Blackbeard. However, he did make his mark in history as a brave and daring man.

CALICO'S CUNNING

In Captain Charles Johnson's book, a General History of the Pirates, a tale is told of Calico Jack stealing a sloop from right under the noses of the Spanish. He and his crew were ashore in Cuba while their small sloop was being refitted. A Spanish warship entered the harbor, bringing with it a captured English sloop. The crew of the Spanish ship caught sight of the pirate ship but the tide was too low for them to make an approach; they would have to wait at the harbor entrance until morning. In the dead of night, Calico Jack and his crew made their way over to the captured English sloop in a rowing boat and overpowered the Spanish guards. At first light, the Spanish warship blasted Calico Jack's sloop with cannon fire, totally unaware that it was empty and the pirate crew was in fact sailing away from the harbor in their captured prize.

Calico Jack and his pirate crewmen eventually accepted the royal pardon from Woodes Rogers in Nassau. The pardon was granted after they claimed they'd been forced into pirating by Charles Vane. However, their attempt to be honest men was short-lived. Calico Jack met Anne Bonny, the wife of a small-time pirate who turned pirate informer for Rogers. They became lovers and Anne tried to have her marriage annulled but her request was denied. She fell pregnant with Jack's baby and went to Cuba to give birth. Soon after, she returned to Nassau without the child; no one is sure what became of it.

Calico Jack soon got restless on land and made the decision to return to a life of piracy. Anne Bonny joined his crew along with several other 'retired' pirates bored of life on shore. One of them was Mary Read, who was dressed as a man. They stole a ship in Nassau and sailed out of the harbor towards the coast of Jamaica where they spent three months attacking fishing boats and fairly insignificant merchant ships.

BONNY AND READ

Legend has it that Anne Bonny, dressed as a man, took a fancy to Mary Read, who was also dressed as a man. Bonny revealed her true identity to Read in an attempt to attract his attention, at which point Read also revealed herself to be a woman. However, there are various other accounts that state both Bonny and Read dressed as women on board the ship, only switching to men's' clothing when they were preparing to fight. It seems unlikely that their true identity was unknown at the time of setting sail and it's quite possible that Bonny and Read knew each other as women before joining Calico Jack's crew… they may even have been lovers.

BONNY'S BACKGROUND

Both women soon gained themselves a reputation for being tough, capable, and often ruthless pirates. They were known to fight, drink and swear every bit, as well as the men and accounts given by fellow crewmen, state that Anne and Mary were bloodthirsty and violent. Where Anne gained her skills is unclear but it's believed she came from Ireland. Her mother is thought to have been a maid who had an affair with her English lawyer employer and the scandal of the affair led to them leaving for America. Anne's father did well in Charleston as a lawyer and he then became a successful merchant, so it was expected that she would settle down and marry a respectable husband. Instead, she fell in love with a sailor who had no means of supporting her. The sailor, James Bonny, quite possibly had his eye on her wealth but her father disinherited her and cast the pair out without a penny.

Anne and James moved to New Providence where James tried his hand at piracy but soon switched his allegiance to making a living collecting bounties for pirates he turned in. It would seem that this switch led to Anne Bonny losing all respect for her husband and she began having affairs, including her affair with Calico Jack.

READ'S BACKGROUND

By the time May Read joined Calico Jack's crew, she was already an experienced pirate crewman. It's believed that she was born in England and grew up dressed as a boy. Her older brother had died and her mother, the widow of a seaman, dressed Mary as a boy so she would receive money from her mother-in-law, Mary's paternal grandmother.

Mary chose to keep her guise as a boy and went on to find work as a soldier. While fighting in Holland for the British, she met a Flemish soldier and revealed her true identity to him. They married and ran an inn together near Breda, but when her husband died Mary returned to life as a soldier.

At the end of the war, Mary was out of work and boarded a ship headed for the West Indies. The ship was captured by pirates and Mary chose to join the pirate crew. She lived a pirate's life in the Caribbean until 1718 when she opted to accept the King's Pardon. Legend has it that Mary was an accomplished fighter. In one story, she had apparently taken a fancy to a man who'd been forced into joining the pirate crew. The man in question was not liked by one of the more ferocious crew members and was challenged to a duel. Fearing that the man she desired might be killed, Mary challenged the cutthroat pirate to a duel herself... and killed him.

After accepting the pardon, Mary found work alongside many other 'retired' pirates on board a privateer ship on a mission to hunt down the pirates who had chosen piracy over the pardon. However, she soon returned to her old ways when the entire crew mutinied and took control of the ship. By 1720 she was part of Calico Jack's pirate crew alongside Anne Bonny.

CALICO CAPTURED

I n the October of 1720, Calico Jack's ship was tracked down by bounty hunters off the coast of Jamaica. Cannon fire was exchanged but the pirate crew had been drinking heavily and it's said that after Jack's ship became damaged, he and his men hid below decks leaving Bonny and Read as the only fighters. The bounty hunters, led by Captain Jonathan Barnet, captured the whole pirate crew and took them to Spanish Town in Jamaica to stand trial.

Calico Jack and all his men were hanged in November, but the execution of Bonny and Read was postponed as both women declared they were pregnant. They were sent to prison but, according to legend, Bonny saw Calico Jack one last time before his hanging and said, "I'm sorry to see you here, but if you had fought like a man, you need not have hanged like a dog."

It's known that Mary Read developed a fever and died in prison a few months later but the fate of Anne Bonny is a mystery. No one knows for sure what became of her but some believe she was eventually freed and, after reconciling with her father, moved back to Charleston where she became a respectable wife and mother until her death in old age. The only thing that's known for sure is that there is no record of her execution.

After his hanging, Calico Jack's corpse was left to rot in a gibbet in an area that's still known as Rackham's Cay today. His career as a pirate was unremarkable but his association with Bonny and Read has ensured his place in pirate folklore.

Chapter Summary

Were all pirates men?

Although they were relatively few in number, some pirates were indeed women. Anne Bonny and Mary Read became the most famous, but neither captained their own ship or made much impact in terms of raids.

Their lasting legacy is the romanticized image of 'girl power' and women making a life for themselves in a man's world.

WHO WAS
JOLLY ROGER?

One other legacy that John 'Calico Jack' Rackham left behind was his flag. In today's world we associate the skull and crossbones image with piracy but in the Golden Age, all pirates had their own distinctive flags. The term "Jolly Roger" is popularly used to describe a white skull and crossbones image on a black flag but pirate ships traditionally raised a solid black or solid red flag to identify themselves as pirates.

Historically, pirate ships attacked under a black flag which conveyed the message that if the ship put up no resistance, everyone on board would be given quarter. If the ship chose to put up a fight, the black flag was replaced with a red flag which sent the message that absolutely no mercy would be shown. These flags were intended to demonstrate the mighty power and fearlessness of the approaching pirate ship and to terrify the targeted ship into surrendering immediately.

THE JOLLY ROGER

Both the solid black and solid red flags were known as the "Jolly Roger" and although there's no documented evidence, it's believed by some that this name originated from the French language term "jolie rouge" which translates as "pretty red".

Another theory is that the name stems from the English term "roger", which was used to describe a "wandering vagabond" or the old English term for the devil which was simply "Old Roger". This theory is backed up by the fact that an image of the devil was a popular addition to many pirate flags.

In Charles Johnson's book of 1724, he documents that both Black Bart and Captain Francis Spriggs used the name "Jolly Roger" to describe their flags but the designs were very different. This generic use has led historians to believe that the term "Jolly Roger" has origins that date further back in history. In fact, records from the 13th century indicate that the image of a skull and crossbones was used by the Knights Templar and then adopted by the Knights of Malta who were known for their acts of piracy.

John Rackham's Flag (top right)

Calico Jack's flag with its image of a white skull over crossed swords on a black background has become synonymous with Golden Age pirate ships and it's the one that's perhaps considered to be the pirate flag in popular culture.

Henry Every's Flag (middle right)

Every's flag was also black and had a white image of a bandana-wearing skull in profile over crossbones.

Blackbeard's Flag (top left)

Blackbeard's black flag had a white image of a horned skeleton holding an hourglass in one hand and spearing a red heart with the other. It was an image designed to strike fear into the hearts of everyone he approached as the hourglass sent the message that time was running out and the speared heart suggested he would show no mercy.

Stede Bonnet's Flag (bottom left)

Bonnet's black flag had a white image of a skull over a bone in the centre with a dagger on one side and a heart on the other.

Emanuel Wynn (middle left)

Emanuel Wynn was an 18th century French pirate and some historians believe he was the first pirate to use the now familiar skull and crossbones image on his black flag. The addition of an hourglass underneath once again sent his victims a clear message that their time was running out if they did not surrender.

BLACK BART'S FLAG

The flag most commonly associated with Black Bart was black with a white image of a skeleton and a pirate holding an hourglass between them. As with Blackbeard's hourglass image, it was designed to send Black Bart's victims the message that time was running out for them.

After his defeat at the hands of ships sent out by the governors of Barbados and Martinique, Black Bart made a special flag that showed an image of him standing on top of two skulls. Under one skull were the letters ABH and under the other, AMH. They stood for "A Barbarian Head" and "A Martinico head".

Thomas Tew (bottom right)

Thomas Tew of Pirate Round infamy is believed to have flown a black flag with a white image of an arm holding a sword. It's thought this image was designed to send out the message that he and his pirate crew were prepared to fight and kill.

Chapter Summary

Who was Jolly Roger?

The Jolly Roger was the name given to the pirate flag and no person named Jolly Roger ever existed. The origins of the name are unclear but it's possible it derived from the French "jolie rouge" which means "pretty red".

WHO WAS THE MOST CUTTHROAT PIRATE OF THEM ALL?

Another pirate flag that struck terror into the hearts of all who saw it approaching was the red skeleton flag of Edward Low. Captain Edward 'Ned' Low was an active pirate in the Caribbean towards the end of the Golden Age. Born in England into poverty, he moved to New England and switched from pick-pocketing to piracy around 1720.

He became a notoriously violent pirate who captured over 100 ships in his three-year career-quite a successful and lengthy career by pirate standards, but his story is retold less often than those of the likes of Blackbeard or Black Bart. The most likely reason for this is his reputation for brutality against his captives and his crew, making him a cold-hearted murderer rather than a romanticized folk hero.

A Maniac And A Brute

Unlike Blackbeard who cultivated a murderous image but apparently never actually harmed any of his captives, Edward Low did harm his captives by violently torturing them before killing them. He was described as "savage and desperate" by author Sir Arthur Conan Doyle and by his own crew as "a maniac and a brute." His acts of cruelty included the following:

- He developed a method of torture that involved tying his victims' hands with rope and weaving it between their fingers before setting it alight and watching it burn away their flesh.

- Fishermen from a captured fishing boat were forced to join his pirate crew; those who refused were kept in chains, whipped and beaten, and constantly threatened with death.

- Two Portuguese passengers found on board a captured English ship were hoisted up and dropped from the yard arm several times until they finally died.

- One victim who escaped gave an account of being beaten before having his ear cut off by Low's cutlass.

- The captain of a captured

Portuguese ship allowed a bag of gold coins to fall overboard rather than fall into Low's hands. As punishment, Low cut off the captain's lips with his cutlass, broiled them, and then forced him to eat them while still burning hot. The rest of the Portuguese crew were then murdered.

• He is reported to have had a French cook burned alive, describing him as "a greasy fellow who would fry well."

• Another tale suggests he used his cutlass to kill 53 captured Spaniards.

• However, after decapitating the captain of a captured fishing boat, his crew refused to carry out his orders to brutally torture the remaining fishermen.

The fate of Edward Low is unclear but one belief is that his crew mutinied after he murdered a sleeping crewman and that he was cast adrift without food or water. After being rescued by a French ship, his identity was discovered and he was hanged in Martinique in 1724. However, others believe that he was never caught and lived the rest of his life in Brazil.

Chapter Summary

So, who was the most cutthroat pirate of them all?

Captain Edward Low was undoubtedly the most brutal and violent pirate of the Golden Age.

Described as a psychopath by historian Edward Leslie, Ned Low will be remembered for his "mutilations, disembowellings, decapitations, and slaughter" more than his acts of piracy.

THE PIRATE LIFESTYLE

Was the pirate way of life something you could handle? What did pirates truly face and how did they live aboard ships and onshore? Fictionalized accounts will tell you they had a romantic life, one desirable by all, but the truth is grimmer. All sailors had trouble sustaining life aboard ships, because of the treacherous weather conditions, fights between attacking ships and poor diet.

LIVING CONDITIONS

The living conditions on-board pirate ships were often better than those on merchant or warships. Conditions below the deck were usually dark, dirty, and damp. The men had to live close together in cramped spaces, often living among rats and eating poorly. Rats were the worst enemies aboard ships because they would eat the food, carry diseases and chew through the ropes.

Pirates had jobs. There were cooks, lookouts, and other pirate positions, so it was not a life of leisure but a life of work to sail the ship. Pirates had to repair the damage to the ships too. Life could be boring in between attacks, but only if the weather was decent. A lot of the time, there were actually too many men on board compared to the amount of work required to run the ship. Chores had to be done then there would be time for singing, playing cards, dancing or sleeping. After an attack, if a ship was captured the extra men would crew the captured ship. At other times, everyone was able to do less on board.

The attire for pirates was anything that was easy to sail in. It needed to be practical and comfortable, but this did not mean it was always in good repair. Men had to care about their clothing to keep it in good form and most didn't; especially with numerous battles to live through.

Ships did not have doctors. Any illness or injury had to be treated by another crew member, and this was not always the best situation. Sometimes the pirates did not survive the journey home due to injury or illness. Their portion of any treasures would go to help bury them. Gold jewelry was often used for funeral services.

DIET

L ife aboard the ship was tough. The food was as scarce as the water. There was only so much space aboard a ship for food storage and only certain foods that could be packed for the long haul. Many sailors and pirates suffered from scurvy because of a lack of fruit. Pirates who remained close to land could stop in and get meals, but for those long sailings across the oceans, food was often limited to salted pork and hard tack.

Salted pork was tough. It was difficult to eat, but at least it provided the necessary protein to the pirates. Hardtack was a hard, long-lasting type of biscuit. Unfortunately, hard tack could be infested with bugs called weevils. If the food ran out, the crew would make soup from boiled bones.

There were some ships that would carry chickens for the eggs and meat that they provided. Of course, the chickens had to be kept alive. The eggs would at least remain fresh and in good supply each day as long as the chickens lived. If the chickens died simply from lack of food they could be eaten, although they would not produce much meat for the pirates.

Fishing for sea creatures was another alternative to gain proper food. Sea turtles, dolphins, and fish could be caught, cooked, and eaten for fresh protein sources. Turtles were specifically desired because they could live aboard for a while until they were needed for food. During the right season, turtle eggs could be obtained from the turtles which provided fresh eggs.

When pirates were not on ships, they typically ate spicy West Indian dishes.

ALCOHOLIC DRINKS

Pirates of fiction are certainly famous for their drinking abilities. According to The Way of the Pirates online version, pirates were known boozers. The evidence states that many pirates needed to prove they had the capacity to drink a lot. The test was usually conducted with beer, and the pirate needed to drink an entire mug full of beer all in one go. Other popular alcoholic drinks included rum, gin and wine. Rum is usually the drink we associate with pirates, again due to fictional accounts.

The truth is a pirate would drink whatever was handy and alcoholic. Sometimes they would mix the various alcohols with different things like lemon juice. The drinks outlined below are made with modern-day ingredients, with an explanation of what was typically used. For example, grenadine syrup would more likely have been cherry juice mixed with sugar.

Bumbo- this is a drink made with dark rum, grated nutmeg or cinnamon, grenadine syrup, and lemon juice.

Flip - this is made with brandy and ale, and also included lemon juice, granulated sugar, egg yolk, and ground ginger.

Sangaree - also known as sangria, is a type of fruit wine, often with lemon or orange pieces mixed in. It is still a very popular drink today.

Rumfustian- this is a combination of sherry, sugar, ale, lemon peel, egg yolk, cinnamon sticks, gin, cloves, and nutmeg.

Grog - this is the most famous of all pirate drinks. It is a hot drink with 2 cans of beer, ½ cup of spiced rum, and a package of oatmeal. Some pirates would finish it with paprika.

When it came to drinking and pirates, some of it was out of necessity that went beyond a drinking test. When out on the open water, the one thing that was often lacking was drinkable water. Pirates, when thirsty, didn't have much choice other than to go to the alcohol supplies aboard ship when there was not enough water. While on board, the pirates did have to limit the amount of drink they had.

A drunken pirate's guard would be down. There

was also the danger of falling on the rigging or running ashore. It was not very smart while on board to relax with alcohol, which may be why they typically got drunk and stayed drunk when on shore. There are numerous accounts that pirates would be aggressive and loud; especially when celebrating. There were times they forced other people to drink too.

HABITS

One habit for early pirates was to just fade into settlements in the Caribbean. They may have gained enough from their campaigns to live an honest life or at least a life off the ship. Some of the pirates would hide within settlements until they were ready to plunder more ships. Quite a few of the early raiders ended up in Jamaica and Haiti, with plenty of land and strongholds to keep themselves safe from those hunting pirate criminals.

Habits and the Daily Routine On Board

- Pirates would work from sun up to sun down on the ships.

- Each day they would rise with daybreak before setting to work for the day.

- Sundays were considered a day of rest, so most pirates could sleep in.

- Crew members slept in hammocks rather than beds.

- Meals on board the ship were designed for morning and late afternoon. The meals would be in a communal kettle. The concept of three daily meals did not exist on a ship due to a lack of food storage.

- Pirates would smoke tobacco. This habit started in childhood and continued until death.

- Pirates had different jobs such as manning the sails and rigging or helping to maintain other equipment on the ship.

- Some of the pirates would keep the armaments in order.

Habits On Shore

Life ashore was different than on the ship. However, it didn't mean that duties were neglected.

- The ships had to be loaded and prepared for the next sailing.

- Pirates would load guns and powder barrels, and bring the heavy cannons on shore when staying in port for a while. These guns were usually put into defensive batteries.

- The sails, blocks, yardarms, and rigging had to be unslung and taken onto the shore. This was a protective method, not only to ensure a ship could not be stolen but also to protect the rigging and sails against inclement weather.

- A lot of the shipboard machinery was also used on land. Typically, it was used with hoists.

- If the area they put into shore was not one they frequented or had been to before, then a campground had to be cleared.

- Pirates would choose the highest point of land for several lookouts to monitor the oceans around the clock.

Pirates didn't want to be besieged with unwanted guests. Pirates could fight pirates, as well as try to pillage and plunder regular people.

- Sleeping pirates hung their hammocks between trees around the campfire.

- Lookouts would be relieved at dawn.

- Once the first meal of the day was over, pirates would go to the ship to work on repairs or cleaning. The equipment was also serviced to make it ready for sailing again.

- Work would typically slow down or stop when the tropical heat was in full swing and would end when it was time for the second meal of the day.

●　Once the second meal was over, it was time for partying, drinking, gambling, plays, music, and other assorted entertainments.

●　If any prisoners were taken, these men would be confined and only let out during the day. There would also be pirates set to watch them throughout the night.

Each captain was different, but many did allow individual pirates to remain around the campfire unsupervised. The details of pirate habits and pirate life described in this section are based on the research conducted by David Marley.

Chapter Summary

What was life like as a pirate?

Most pirates had it better than when they were merchant or military sailors, but life was still not perfect.

Captains instilled the rules that each pirate had a job or duty to perform throughout the day. These duties varied and only two meals were ever given each day, along with something to drink whether it was water or alcohol.

THE DIFFERENT TYPES OF PIRATE SHIPS

Given the length of time, pirates have been around plundering and pillaging, it should not come as a surprise that there were various styles of pirate ships. Each ship had main characteristics that set it apart from other ships of the 17th and 18th centuries.

BARK

Bark, usually spelled Barque in Old English, was a fast, light ship with a shallow draft. Pirates favored this ship because it was designed to be small and quick and capable of coming upon slower ships with ease. The bark was a three-mast-ship with square sails. The mizzen mast was the only one that was not square. The Bark was used throughout the 1800s. The ship usually weighed 500 tons and carried 100 men. Other versions of this ship could have four or five masts and be larger.

BRIG

The brigs were smaller ships than the barks. They were typically 150 to 250 tons capacity. The brig was one of the fastest pirate ships and most desired because it had top maneuverability. The ship did need skilled men to sail it. The brig usually had two masts, with square sails. The main mast also tended to have fore and aft sails, which made it perfect for almost all wind conditions. At one point shipbuilders had a brig-schooner, where the main mast was "lateen-rigged."

CARAVEL

The Caravel was an original ship designed in the 15th century and used well into the 17th century. The ship was crafted for Mediterranean sailing, with lateen rigging or sails in the shape of a triangle. The Spanish and Portuguese changed the original Caravel to have three masts. The first two masts had square sails, and the third aft mast had lateen sails. A few of the historical Caravel ships had four masts. Like the brig, they were small-in fact, smaller than the brig. These ships had 80 to 130 tons capacity and were only 75 feet in length. The hulls were shallow to ensure that long explorations of coasts could be conducted. The drawback for pirates was the small living quarters and cargo capacity.

CARRACK

The Carrack was a merchant ship built in the 15th and 16th centuries. In the 16th century, the Carrack design was changed to include equipment that would defend against pirates. These ships had guns mounted. It was the first of its type. The guns were in the lower hull. The Carracks changed from merchant ships to warships. They were also large at over 1,000-ton capacity. The new ships were built with three or four masts, but there were some with two masts. The Carrack had topsails, which were on the main and fore masts. The stern was built to support a large crew, as well as an area for fighting.

Given the guns and the size of these ships, pirates desired them. They had their own weapons, so when possible they would attack Carrack ships for the goods on board and the ship. When they captured these ships, they would repair them if possible, and add them to their fleet. Not every captain was the same, thus not every captain would have a fleet. It was also possible to sell the ships or strip them of their armaments. Depending on the pirate ship or the damage the pirate ship might have sustained, there were also times when Carrack warships became the new pirate ship for the group.

DUTCH FLUTE

Starting in the 17th century the Dutch flute was the most popular ship, at least in European waters. The Dutch flute usually had three masts with two square riggings and a lateen-rigged to the mizzenmast.

The Dutch flute became the largest cargo carrier and the most common on the high seas. The design of the ship was simple, making it an affordable option to build. It did not require a large crew either, which is why they were easy to obtain. Pirates tended to attack this type of ship, take it to a nearby port, take everything off of it and either destroy it or sell it. Most Dutch flutes were 80 feet long and 300 tons.

FRIGATE

Frigate ships were built as medium-sized warships, with a weight of 1,000 tons. The first frigates appeared in the 17th century. The forecastle and quarterdeck were raised, and the ship had three masts with all square sails. Since it was a warship, anywhere from 24 to 40 guns would be mounted on the 2.5 gun decks. Some versions even had 70 guns. These ships were designed for patrolling, escorting other ships, shore bombardment, and scouting. The idea was for these ships to be able to defend and hunt pirates. Anywhere from 50 to 200 crew could fit on a frigate. The frigate was built with speed and agility, but against ship-of-the-line warships that pirates had the frigates usually lost. Gaining a frigate and selling its parts or keeping it was also something pirates did. Most often, they would take the guns, and make a profit off everything else they didn't need.

GALLEON

Like a few of the other ships, the Galleon was made in the 15th through to the 17th centuries. You probably recognize the name as a Spanish Galleon, rather than just a Galleon. The Spanish designed and developed this ship as their main treasure and merchant transporter. Pirates would attack these ships for large cargo. Speed was definitely a part of the ship's design, along with 500 tons storage capacity. Most of the galleons you will see in museums or pictures will have three masts, with two square sail riggings and a triangle on the stern mast. To prevent pillage and plundering, the decks were outfitted with 70 to 100 guns. The sailor's hold or poop deck could contain 200 to 400 sailors. The Galleon to some scholars was an upgrade to the caravel ship. As a ship with a large capacity, it was another desired by pirates not only to sell it to someone else but to outfit it as a pirate ship.

GALLEY

The Galley ship probably has the longest history when it comes to pirates. The Galley was built between the 15th and 16th centuries, often for use on the Barbary Coast. The Galley was designed to have less width, with a longer length. These ships had at least one mast, with lateen sails. Yet the speed was not from the wind in the sails, but the oars used to row the ship. When used by countries, slaves or convicts would row the ship. For pirates, it was all about the crew of the ship. They would jail or lock up the crew, use them to power the ship, and loot the ship. If a pirate did use the galley style, then they would have a pirate crew to row the ship until they found crew from another ship to enslave for the rowing. A galley had one deck only. It also had a shallow draft, making it a good ship for traveling close to the coast. At least 100 or more pirates were needed to overpower a crew of the galley. Adventure Galley is probably the most famous of these ships, which was run by Captain William Kidd in the late 1600s.

SCHOONER

Schooners were definitely popular ships in the Caribbean. As you study the history of specific pirates, you will notice that the schooner tended to be a favorite among most pirates. Schooners were built to be fast, with a narrow hull compared to other ships. Schooners could only carry 100 tons, but they had speed and agility beyond most of the other ships. It could reach 11 knots with the right wind. Only 75 men could be on board, and there was room for 8 to 12 guns. The narrow, flat hull also made it easy to get into the shallow waters or shoals of the Caribbean, and attack and escape with ease. Most schooners were built with two masts; however, some versions did have three or four masts. The downside to schooners was the cruising range. A long trek in a schooner meant starvation, thus pirates had to stick near islands and other land masses for safety.

SHIP OF THE LINE

In the 16th through the 18th centuries, ship-of-the-line style ships were built. These were huge warships that could overpower all other ships. In design, they mirrored the frigate, except for the luxury and the expensive costs to build one. Skilled sailors had to be on board these ships, usually 850 men at least. The entire ship had 100 guns mounted on the decks. There could be two to four decks of guns. The weight of this ship was usually 1,000 tons. As usual, it was a three-masted ship, with square rigging and a mizzen mast with fore and aft sails. Countries built the ship-of-the-line as battleships to counterattack pirates. However, it did not mean the ship would always be the winner. Pirates were cunning and sneaky, and according to The Way of the Pirates online resource, able to take some of these ships.

SLOOP

The sloop was desired like the schooner because of its 11-knot speed. It was highly agile and built with a shallow hull for getting into the shoals and shallow waters. Sloops were built with oars to help increase their speed. For speedy pirate action, the sloop was considered best. It was built with one or two masts, with a fore and aft rigging style. Typically, there was one mast with one jib for speed. The pirate crew contained 75 men, along with 14 mounted guns. Sloops had 100 tons capacity and 60 feet of length. When the navy started building ships, the sloop became bigger and upgraded to have more mounted guns.

SNOW

The Snow was another ship with two masts that were used for more than one century. The weight of the ship was about 1,000 tons. It was nearly identical in design to the brig; however, it had fore and main square masts, along with a trysail mast to help keep the ship moving in a storm. Snow ships were built for battle and merchant services, with a capacity to carry 80 men. Often 10 cannons were mounted on the ship, which had one gun deck. The snows were built for the British Royal Navy for pirate hunting, but that didn't mean pirates didn't gain control of these ships.

THE MOST FAMOUS PIRATE SHIPS

- The Queen Anne's Revenge is considered the most famous pirate ship throughout history. Blackbeard's Queen Anne's Revenge was a 300-ton frigate. It held 26 guns when it was taken from a French captain. Blackbeard outfitted it with 40 guns and carried 150 crewmen.

- Fancy was Henry Every's ship. This ship was called a man of war with 46 cannons and 150 men on board. The man of war had a poop deck, quarter deck, forecastle, upper, middle, and lower deck, orlop deck, and hold. This type of construction was a three-masted ship for the navy. It was fast but larger, with a lot of water displacement making it less easy to crew than a schooner or smaller ship.

- William Kidd's ship was a Galley, at 284 tons with 34 cannons and 100 crewmen.

- The Golden Hind was another famous ship. It was a galleon-style ship with a 100-ton capacity and 18 guns mounted.

- Captain John Gow had a merchant ship. This was a merchant class of ship that was more like the Dutch flute, capable of carrying passengers and cargo.

- Calico Jack sailed a sloop, as did Tomas Tew and Charles Vane. They were named William, Liberty and the Amity, and Ranger respectively. The ranger was a sloop capable of carrying 10 cannons and 60 men. Calico Jack's ship only had 6 cannons according to historical research by Brethren Coast.

- Edward England also captained a galley, three of them called Fancy, Victory, and Royal James.

- Bartholomew Roberts captained the Royal Fortune, Great Ranger, and Great Fortune. Roberts captained a brig and a warship. Roberts was also said to have a ship called the Little Ranger, with 10 cannons, but the type is unknown. Royal Fortune was a frigate.

PIRATE TACTICS WITH SHIPS

Pirates looted ships. They ran other ships aground, boarded them, and often captured the crew, but what were their tactics? Was it like in the movies where pirate ships were faster or were there just a bunch of gunfire until someone surrendered? Ship-capturing techniques did vary according to the situation. Scholars are also divided on the exact tactics used due to various accounts and tall tales. Legends held a lot of power in the earlier centuries when fear and misunderstanding could be used to one's advantage. For example, many scholars believe Blackbeard lit his beard on fire or at least lit some TNT fuses on fire that was tied to his hair to create an element of fear. The following are most likely the tactics used by pirates.

- The pirates sailing the shipping lanes would find a target. In earlier days the pirates wouldn't have had to worry about Navy ships; however as stricter laws were enforced by many gunned navy ships, pirates had to be smarter. Pirates tended to stay in familiar waters so they could find unprotected targets, such as the merchant ship taking a non-popular route to avoid pillaging and plundering. Pirates tried to avoid navy ships unless there was no other course of action. It also depended on how badly the crew was starving, with regard to finding an acceptable target.

● The larger ships required more caution before approaching. Frigate-sized ships could be detrimental to their own small crew and firepower. Shadowing the target and observing and finding the best way to approach without notice was often the tactic used on larger ships. When an opportunity to advance and board occurred the pirates would take it, after observation.

● Advancing on the larger ship or any vessel had to be stealthy, until the pirate ship was close enough to fire warning shots, use scare tactics and employ other methods. There were times when pirates would raise false colors or distress flags to try to trick other captains. However, it didn't always work and thus was more of a last resort. Most pirates would sail in, fire warning shots, and use crew fears as a method of getting the other ship to surrender. Sometimes the pirate, if he was on a faster ship, would approach quickly so he was ready for action if the captain didn't surrender.

- When merchants were caught by surprise they would, about 60 to 70 percent of the time, just surrender. However, if the merchant knew the pirate was coming they would prepare for combat. When warning shots and scare tactics were used, captains typically surrendered. It was easier to surrender and live another day than to fight it out. Historical records show quite a few merchants would bribe or at least attempt to bribe the pirates. It could work with pirates hoping for food and money to spend. Depending on the value of the cargo, some captains had to fight to protect it.

- If fighting occurred, the pirates would do their best to quickly disable the crew. Various tactics would be used to convince the crew. An unhappy crew isn't about to lose their life for their captain, so surrender of the crew worked in some instances. When this did work the guns and other weapons would be unmanned. If a pirate did not surprise another ship and was unable to talk the crew into surrendering, the crew and the pirates would have to fight. There were times when the crew would be larger than the pirates expected, which would cause a large, fire-powered fight to break out. Casualties on both sides would occur. Ships on both sides could be damaged. Some merchant ships might be able to get away, but in most instances, the pirate ships were faster.

• Both ship captains knew that disabling the sails and rigging was the best way to disable the ship if disabling the crews did not work. Pirates would often fire at the sails and rigging to try to disable it. In some cases, they would get close enough to the merchant ship to board it and send pirates up the rigging to disable the ship. The captain of merchant ships had to determine if surrendering was best based on the issues with disabling the crew and ship. Surrendering could have meant retaining one's life. The pirate code you read about above clearly shows that prisoner policies were more acceptable for the crew and captains to surrender rather than fight.

• When a ship was boarded either by force or by surrender, there were still things that had to be taken care of. First, the pirates had to determine if they would board by boat or if they needed grappling hooks to board safely.

• If the crew did surrender, then those who chose to join the pirate crew would be allowed to roam free. If other passengers or crew did not surrender, then they would be taken as prisoners.

• As soon as the crew was dealt with, the prize- whether it was the ship, cargo or another prize would be taken to the port where it could be sold for money.

PRISONERS-PASSENGERS AND CREW

Pirate police would limit the amount of new crew that could become pirates. Often pirates were looking for crew members that would be beneficial. Crew, such as carpenters, coopers, surgeons, and other skilled crew members could be very helpful for pirate crews. They could help make things, help injured pirate crew, and generally lend skills to the ship.

Scholars differ on this next point, but there are records stating that other crew and passengers were either sold into slavery or ransomed. Those who disagree that slavery and ransom were indeed pirate trades feel there is a lack of evidence to support these claims and that most of them have been fictionalized. However, there is sufficient evidence from personal stories which are now in museums that lend to the truth that slavery and ransomed actually occurred.

Not every passenger on a merchant or passenger ship would be someone to ransom. High-valued passengers, usually easy to pick out from the rest because of their rooms on the ship and the items packed with them, would be ransomed back to their families. They were kept for a short time in a group until the ransom notes could reach their families. If the passenger had enough funds on them, they could also pay for their freedom.

Passengers and crew who could not pay would either be let go at the next port or be sold into slavery. It depended on whether the market was right. If there was no one in need of slaves, then there was nothing to be gained by trying to sell the crew and passengers. If the cargo could be loaded onto their own ship, then the pirates would sometimes leave the ship and crew installed.

If the ship, crew, and unworthy passengers were left behind, they usually needed to fix the ship before they could sail. It would not do for the ship to sail right into the next port along with the pirates.

Chapter Summary

Were all of the ships listed in this chapter pirate ships?

Yes and no- some ships were outfitted for merchants and navy, but pirates captured them, kept them or sold them.

The best naval ship was the ship-of-the-line, in terms of naval warships. For pirates, the schooner was one of the fastest and most agile against any of the merchant or warships. The schooner could handle a few cannons, but not nearly as many as the larger warships. There was often a need to take large ships with the pirates to get the cargo to shore and sell it.

WHO WAS WHO
ON PIRATE SHIPS

Every ship needed to have a crew. There were also jobs to be done not only during sailing, but also when in port. Discovering who was who on a ship could be a little more daunting than you realize. After reading about some of the pirate codes and articles, you are aware that pirates could mutiny to elect a new captain or choose a new captain and ship by pledging allegiance to those codes and articles. The outline here is about positions, how one was either elected or was asked to fill that position, and why they might be put into those particular "jobs."

CAPTAIN

Pirate captains were democratically elected. These captains could be replaced at any time; particularly if there was a reason for mutiny or a new majority vote to be held. Some captains were voted out because they were not aggressive enough in the pursuit of cargo and other goods. Other captains were too aggressive, brutal or bloodthirsty for the crew to feel safe. Captains were meant to be bold, decisive, and skillful. A captain had to be able to lead the crew, navigate and run the ship with respect. Captains needed to retain their abilities and treat the crew well, but mostly ensure that they were providing enough money to the crew to keep them happy. If a captain wasn't getting the job done, he could be removed from his position and in some situations murdered.

THE QUARTERMASTE R

The quartermaster was nearly on the same level as the captain; especially during the Golden Age of Piracy. The captain could have unlimited authority during any battle; however, at all other times the quartermaster was a kind of "cop." He was the regulator, the person who would punish for minor offenses and if necessary overrule the captain. The quartermaster was also an elected person. He would maintain order, distribute food and essentials and settle any quarrel. The crew had to vote if any flogging was to happen, but otherwise, for minor issues, the quartermaster did not need permission. Most quartermasters kept records, including the account books. When there were boarding parties, the quartermaster was usually the leader. He would be the man to decide what cargo to take. The crew would have to vote on whether a captured ship would be kept, it was then that the quartermaster would take over as captain of the new ship.

SAILING MASTER

The sailing master, also known as the navigator, was an officer in rank on a pirate ship. This person would keep the boat on course and look at the maps and instruments. The navigator had a difficult time because maps during the age of piracy were often incorrect. A great navigator was considered "worth his weight in gold." One might even say the navigator was more valuable than any other person on that ship since it was his job to make sure the boat safely returned to port or came across a ship they could rob. Most of the navigators working aboard a pirate vessels were forced into that service. Others were elected to be captains and navigators.

BOATSWAIN

The boatswain was also valuable to the ship. This person would oversee the maintenance of the ship, as well as the supply stores. The boatswain would inspect the ship before it sailed, the rigging each day in the morning and would then report the condition of all to the captain. Deck activities were all under the purview of the boatswain. He would say when to weigh or drop anchor, as well as the handling of all the sails.

MASTER GUNNER

The master gunner was responsible for all guns and ammunition. The master gunner had to make sure the powder was dry and prevent it from separating. He also had to maintain the cannon balls, so they were be free of rust. All weapons that were not personal weapons were also under his guidance, since he would need to ensure the condition of them. The master gunner's intelligence about weapons was necessary for the safety of all crew, as well as the effectiveness of the weapons.

CARPENTER

Most ships had a carpenter. Like the boatswain, this person would be responsible for maintenance, but it was directed more toward the repair and maintenance of the wooden hull, yards, and masts. Typically, the carpenter was under the direct supervision of the boatswain and/or ship's master. The carpenter would look at the hull regularly. Sometimes this person would have to put oakum between the plank seams and around wooden plugs to ensure the vessel would not leak. Most carpenters were apprentices of another carpenter. Often an assistant would be trained, and then find a new boat or take over the carpenter position when the last one left the ship or died.

MATE

The mate was in a higher position than a sailor. It was the term used to signify that a person was under training or was an apprentice of a skilled person on the ship. The mate could serve the boatswain, the ship's master, the gunner, or the carpenter. Depending on the position, the mate would ensure the vessel was outfitted- he would examine the ropes, sails, pulleys, and other rigging. The mate could be in charge of actually hoisting the anchor. Most mates would see to the tackle used for fishing, and other tackle on board. If the mate found anything incorrect, he would bring the problem to his master or the ship's master. During port returns, the mate would usually take anchors and cables to be repaired. He might also manage the sails, the mooring of the ship, and the yards.

SAILOR

Sailors were the rest of the crew. These individuals would operate the ship on a daily basis, ensuring the sails and rigging were in working order. For example, if the sails needed to be raised a team of sailors would see to it. If the boat was going into a port, the sailors would need to work the sails and rigging to ensure the captain could put the ship safely into port. Sailors would sometimes steer the ship, as well as listen to the navigator to make sure the voyage was going in the right direction.

The sailor had to understand the winds, the skies, the weather, and the moods of all commanders.

SURGEON

Some pirate ships took on surgeons. Often these individuals were forced into the work like navigators. Surgeons were skilled and therefore they didn't need to work as pirates, but if they were found on a larger ship then they were made to be in service. Large pirate ships were typically the vessels they worked on.

COOK

The cook could be a sailor or another among the crew, but on larger vessels, there was a specific person for cooking.

CABIN BOY

Cabin boys were young sailors, often apprentices learning how to sail.

Positions could change if someone became sick or died, such as mates learning how to be boatswains, carpenters or navigators. A cabin boy would eventually become a sailor, who may rise in the ranks eventually to captain. It all depended on how long one could remain alive sailing and pillaging other ships.

Chapter Summary

Who was the most important person on a pirate ship?

You now know that the navigator was considered the most important person due to his skill. The navigator could be the captain or the ship's master. It would depend on who was elected as the captain and whether that person had navigation skills.

The crew was also made up of various apprentices and commanders who would help keep the ship in shape, so sailors could guide it through the waters and into port.

TYPES OF PIRATE WEAPONS AND AMMUNITION

The life of the pirate started to get more difficult when Navy ships and other law enforcement measures were put in place to stop the plundering and pillaging. These changes meant an increase in the use of weapons during the 16th century. By the 17th century, pirates had numerous weapons, including cannons that they would use. These weapons ensured they were able to raid more successfully, as well as hold captives more securely. The downside to pirate weapons and ammunition was that the merchant ships and warships were carrying the same types of weapons. No one had more advanced weapons than anyone else. It is why some of the tactics mentioned in a previous chapter were employed. It was always more useful to have people surrender rather than engage in a weapon-led battle.

PERSONAL WEAPONS

Each pirate had their own preferences for weaponry. There were various knives, pistols, swords, and two-handed guns for personal use.

Pirate Knives

Knives, dirks, daggers, and machetes were popular sharp weapons for pirates. In the case of close combat, knives were the best weapon to remain agile. Several pirates had what were considered short swords; they had shorter blades than a sword but longer blades than the average knife. The idea of knives was to ensure the weapon was an extension of the body, while keeping the pirate's body away from any weapon on the opposing side. Another reason for knives was the small decks and holds the pirates would have to fight in.

Pirate Swords

The cutlass was the most popular weapon for pirates. Pirates who wanted a better chance at fighting without injury often used swords. Their length was better than knives, but it also meant more power was needed to wield them. Rapiers were also common swords. Rapiers had a narrower blades compared with the cutlass. Cavalry sabers were less used given the single edge and design; however, some military men turned pirates would use these sabers. They got used to the style of the sword. Broadswords were the most unwieldy in comparison to all other swords. They were longer than the other swords and were also double-bladed. Pirates typically wanted quick thrusting action with the swords rather than a heavy double-bladed sword.

Pirate Guns

Most of the guns required two hands to fire. Musket rifles, musketoons and blunderbusses were extremely popular among the pirates for long-range fighting. They were also about the only guns besides the pistols available during the pirates plundering and pillaging. Musket rifles were a simple design, with a long barrel. They required front loading with gunpowder and a lead bullet, then a fuse to fire them. Musketoons were a smaller weapon, with less accuracy. This type of weapon was only useful when fighting in tight corridors. With a tight space, the person pirates were aiming at had fewer places to hide and thus the pirates could often hit their target.

The blunderbuss is one of the more popular fictional pirate weapons and it was definitely a real weapon. Think of the blunderbuss as the modern-day shotgun. It was a shorter rifle barrel, but with better accuracy than the musketoon.

Pirate Pistols

Pistols were smaller, shorter barrel weapons. They were light and easy to carry into any situation. It didn't mean the accuracy or usage was as easy as today; however, they could do quite a bit of damage when used in close quarters. The Flintlock pistol was the most common. It still needed to be loaded from the front, but the top part of the gun had flint which would be struck hard when the trigger was pulled. This created a fire spark that would shoot the bullet at the adversary. Multi-barrel pistols were also highly common and useful because they had a better firing rate. Instead of one shot, you would get two before needing to reload the gun. The third most popular weapon for pistols was the volley. The volley had several barrels which fired at the same time, rather than being able to fire from one barrel and then the other like the multi-barrel pistols. The idea was to create as much damage in one shot as possible to stop the rest of the crew from continuing or at least getting the upper hand against the pirates.

Boarding Pikes

Guns, pistols, knives, and swords might have been

a part of the personal armor as fighting weapons, but pirates also needed other more exotic weapons for their fighting situations. For example, the boarding pike was able to be used not only to board another ship but also to be thrown a short distance and fend off any swordmen in the crew. The boarding axe was similar. It would be used for climbing the side of the ship, cutting through hatches, doors, and rigging, and if necessary killing or injuring any crewmen that got too close.

Pirate Cannons

Pirate cannons were not personal weapons, but the ship's weapons. Pirate ships had cannons of less than 700 kilograms and 8-pound balls. These were the shorter barrel cannons. Pirates needed lighter cannons than those found on most warships because they were heavy and unwieldy. The cannons would sail back after being shot, so a person had to be out of the way. They would then be loaded again with a heavy ball and pushed forward to aim.

Cannons were also hard to come by in the 17th century. It was not until the 18th century that nearly every ship had cannons. There were numerous styles of cannons, some of which the pirates took from other ships and others cannons that they bought and weaponized their ships with. Most of the cannons required at least 6 men to operate them. The original cannons were made from bronze, but as technology improved so did the ability to use iron for a faster, more accurate shot. The two most popular cannons on pirate ships were as follows:

Carronade

The Carronade was not built until 1778. It was a product of the Scottish Carron Company. More often, pirates would get these cannons from the Royal Navy ships they plundered. The cannons were short-range, with a powerful ability to damage anything in their way. Carronades would destroy ships with cannon balls. Since pirates did not want to destroy the ship they intended on selling, they often had these guns more for the threat than the damage they could cause.

Swivel Gun

Swivel guns were the smallest cannons. They were lighter and easier to mount or unmount from pirate ships. This made the swivel gun the more desirable weapon for the ship. The main purpose of swivel guns was to kill any of the crew or people before boarding, rather than to destroy the ship. Since the cannons were mounted on a swivel-style stand, they had a wider range and more mobility. They also worked very well for keeping another crew from boarding the pirate ship. Swivel guns could fire various ammunition as well as the favored grapeshot. The downside was low accuracy. A pirate ship had to get in close before it could hit a target perfectly, which in some ways could be dangerous.

AMMUNITION

As there were various weapons to use against ship crews, there were also numerous types of ammunition.

- The Bundle shot was fashioned with several pieces of metal. These metal pieces were then connected via rope. The rope would open, allowing the metal to spread. If the metal hit something, the rope twisted around the target and could cause destruction or death. Think of the bundle shot as a hollow point bullet that fragments upon entering the body.

- The chain and bar shot had two halves of a ball. They were connected with a bar or chain. The Navy designed these bullets or shots to ruin rigging, sails, and masts. When shot, they had enough force to blast through wood masts or rip through sails. Pirates also used this type of shot when they managed to get them from the navy because the shot was effective in rendering a ship dead in the water.

- Canister or Grapeshot was used in cannons. They were small iron balls meant to destroy anything close by. The grape shot was more damaging than the canister, which was an iron ball in an iron box that would explode after it left the cannon barrel.

- Explosive shells and hot iron were used as hollow type of cannon balls. Inside the cannonball gunpowder would be placed, along with a small fuse. Pirates had to be careful because the wrong move or a too-long fuse could make it go off before the pirate was ready. The hot iron shot was slightly different. It was a bar of red hot iron used to put an enemy ship on fire.

- Round shot was the most basic iron ball used with cannons. It was light enough to go a medium shooting distance. Unfortunately, they were hard to aim, pirates typically used them for land fortifications and destruction.

- Sangrenel was considered anti-personnel ammunition. It was a cloth bag that held metal balls, shavings, and iron scraps. It could be fired from cannons with devastating effects. The bag would usually rip as it snagged on something ensuring the metal pieces would be embedded in the ship, and people, or destroy the sails and rigging.

Chapter Summary

Weapons helped solve some of the fighting issues and ensured surrender, correct?

The short answer is yes; however one must realize that merchant and warship captains had weapons too. If a pirate did not surprise the crew, then the threat of readied weapons was often enough to get a surrender. If the captain had time to prepare their own cannons and personal weapons, then a fight was more likely to ensue.

DID PIRATES
HAVE PARROTS?

A nyone attending a fancy-dress party dressed as a pirate today will undoubtedly have a stuffed parrot named Polly attached to the shoulder of their costume, but did pirates really have parrots?

Well, the answer is yes and no: pirates did catch parrots and keep them on their ships, but they rarely kept them as pets. During the Golden Age of Piracy exotic pets were highly sought after in Europe, so pirates captured parrots on the Caribbean islands and pretty much named their price at the next port. Pretty Polly wasn't a pet, she was a means of making money.

WHAT ABOUT PEG LEGS?

Another popular addition to a modern-day pirate costume is a peg leg, so did pirates really have wooden legs?

It wasn't uncommon for a pirate to lose a limb in battle, but survival was also fairly uncommon. In an attempt to survive infection or gangrene injured limbs would often be cut off, but as the 'surgery' would generally be performed by the ship's cook rather than a doctor, bleeding to death was a more likely outcome than surviving long enough to need a peg leg. However, if a prosthetic was needed, wood was the obvious choice as it was readily available aboard a wooden ship.

Chances of survival were higher for amputated hands but the loss of a limb generally ended a pirate's career as life on the ocean wave was no place for an incapacitated crewman. Our modern-day image of pirate ships crewed by peg-legged and hook-fisted crewmen is an image that has grown out of works of fiction.

BUT DID THEY WEAR BANDANAS AND GOLD EARRINGS?

Yes, they did. Pirates would often wear bandanas simply to protect themselves from the sun, but keeping their hair under wraps also prevented it from accidentally getting caught up in the ship's ropes and pulleys.

It was a common tradition for young sailors to be presented with gold earrings as a mark of their first sailing across the equator or around Cape Horn, but many pirates wore them for superstitious reasons. Some believed that precious metals contained magical healing powers and that wearing a gold earring would either protect their eyesight or cure poor eyesight. Another common belief was that a gold earring protected the wearer from drowning, but of course in reality plenty of earring-wearing pirates found their eyesight deteriorating or did indeed drown. However, the value of a gold earring was enough to pay for a man's funeral and it was common practice among seafarers to have the name of their home port engraved on the inside of their earring so that their body could be returned to home soil rather than being buried at sea.

AND EYE PATCHES?

There's no documented evidence to support the idea that pirates wore eye patches but there is a theory that some may have done so in an effort to keep themselves prepared for changing light conditions in a battle situation. With one eye covered in sunlight, they'd always have one eye adjusted to dark conditions if they had to go below deck. By simply removing the eye patch, they'd instantly be able to see rather than having to wait for their eyes to adjust from light to dark.

DID PIRATES MAKE THEIR VICTIMS WALK THE PLANK?

Although there are some accounts of pirates forcing their captives to walk the plank, it's unlikely to have been a common occurrence. In 1829, Dutch crewmen on a captured ship were made to walk the plank with cannonballs tied around their ankles. However, there are very few such cases that can be supported by any kind of historical documentation. It's now believed that walking the plank may have been used occasionally as a form of entertainment by the more sadistic of pirate crewmen but, on the whole, pirates tended to grab a captured ship's loot and run.

And did they say, "Arrr, me hearties!" and

"Shiver me timbers!"?

In the 1950s, an actor named Robert Newton played the role of Long John Silver in Disney's adaptation of Treasure Island, written by Robert Louis Stevenson in 1883. His image, accent, and mannerisms in the role pretty much set the standard for the traditional 'pirate image' we continue to recreate in fancy dress costumes today. So did pirates say, "Arrr, me hearties!"? Only fictional ones in films were created long after the Golden Age of Piracy.

WHAT ABOUT BURIED TREASURE?

Captain William Kidd is the only pirate known to have buried any treasure. The idea of a treasure map with an 'X' marking the spot is once again the stuff of fictional novels and films. Pirates kept their treasure on board their ships and enjoyed spending it at every opportunity.

DID PIRATES USE TREASURE MAPS?

Again, this is mostly fictional. Pirates kept their "booty" aboard to spend it, thus there was not a real need to have a treasure map. Captain William Kidd was the only one to bury his treasure. Paul Hawkins has debated the fact that Captain Kidd had maps. The British Museum or at least an employee of the museum was said to have tested four maps: Saga, Key, Bureau, and Morgan maps. However, there is nothing on record indicating these tests. Skelton, the employee, did report the ink and parchment to have appropriate 17th-century origins. There are also documents with a British Museum stamp on them, but no records for those tests. The maps in question are related more to sailing around the oceans than to actual treasure.

PIRATES' WHO'S WHO – PIRATE BIOGRAPHIES AT A GLANCE

Name: John Rackham

Pirate name: Calico Jack

Ships: Kingston (unnamed others)

Years active: 1718 - 1720

Claim to fame: Association with female pirates Anne Bonny and Mary Read

Name: Edward Teach

Pirate name: Blackbeard

Ships: Queen Anne's Revenge, Adventure

Years active: 1716 - 1718

Claim to fame: Most feared pirate in the Caribbean;

terrifying image

Name: Bartholomew Roberts

Pirate name: Black Bart

Ships: Royal Rover, Good Fortune, Royal Fortune, Ranger, Little Ranger

Years active: 1719 - 1722

Claim to fame: Captured over 400 ships

Name: Henry Every

Pirate name: Long Ben

Ships: Fancy

Years active: 1694 - 1696

Claim to fame: Captured the Ganj-i-Sawai and vanished without trace

Name: William Kidd

Pirate name: Captain William Kidd

Ships: Adventure Galley, Adventure Prize, Antonio

Years active: 1696 - 1701

Claim to fame: Pirate hunter turned pirate; buried treasure

BLACKBEARD: THE PIRATE TERROR OF THE SEA

INTRODUCTION

First of all, I would like to say thank you for purchasing this book, "Blackbeard: A Pirate Terror of the Sea". I believe you will find here a comprehensive knowledge of one of history's most revered outlaws. Do you find yourself strangely drawn to current books, films, and other popular culture references to pirates? I'm sure you are familiar with the book "Treasure Island" or the Pirates of the Caribbean movie series, right? Well, you would probably be surprised to know that most if not all of these fictional accounts were loosely based on one man. Blackbeard. In the following chapters, we will discuss the man and the legend who was a defining personality during the Golden Age of Piracy and maritime history, in general.

Before we dive in, I'd like you to imagine yourself aboard the deck of a French merchant ship in the year 1718. You have just spent two seasons sailing across the Atlantic to trade for cocoa and sugar in the Caribbean and now are completing your journey on the Gulf Stream back home. The Americas dipped below the horizon and into the sea a few days ago. Almost to the final waypoint in Bermuda, the sun begins to set. In the dim light of dawn, another ship appears visible through the fog. As it draws nearer, you are able to distinguish a familiar flag through a hand-held brass monocular. The sky continues to darken and the vessel inches closer. Something wasn't right. A small Spanish sloop out in the middle of the ocean?

Curiosity morphs into a panic when at the last moment, a new flag is hoisted; A tattered, black cloth bearing a white skeleton. Pirates. Through the gun ports in the side of the tiny sloop, three cannon muzzles appear. Dozens of armed men stand at the ready. The booming explosion of a warning shot cuts through the night and a flash of firelight briefly illuminates the grey sky. Not long after, you find yourself in the crossfire of pistols, cannons, and grenades. Hordes of men climb over the gunwales and onto the deck swinging cutlasses and axes and seizing the members of your crew. Amid the chaos and through the billows of smoke, you catch a glimpse of a truly otherworldly figure. He stands tall behind his men. His wiry black hair smoldering underneath a large, black captain's hat; and black ribbons sway from braids in his beard. His broad chest is adorned with holsters stuffed full of pistols and cutlasses. Blackbeard has just pirated another ship.

CHAPTER 1: SPECULATION CONCERNING THE EARLY LIFE OF EDWARD TEACH

T he details of Edward Teach's early life are shrouded in mystery and largely left to speculation. Alternate spellings of his surname, Thack or Thatch, have been disputed by scholars and historians for years. Taking into account the customs of sailors during the Golden Age of Piracy in the Caribbean, his true name will quite probably never be known. Accounts of his early life and career have long been entangled with embellishment and propaganda and serve to consistently perplex researchers. The general consensus, however, is that Teach was born in what is now Bristol sometime around the year 1680. During the 17th and 18th century, the rise of the American colonies and the Atlantic slave trade transformed Bristol into a bustling seaport. The author Robert Lee has suggested that Teach was likely born to a wealthy and respected family who afforded their son the education to read and write. One of the only legitimate clues about the life of Edward Teach is a curious book entitled "A General History of the Robberies and Murders of the Most Notorious Pyrates", published in 1724 under a pseudonym. The book in and of itself has been likened to a treasure map which at times led enthusiasts down a dead-end path and proved to be a complete fabrication. Other times, that path revealed a treasure chest of verifiable fact which is backed by government accounts and has served most subsequent publications on the topic. Through recent years, however, researchers have begun to unearth other accounts contained in English, French, and American archives. According to underwater explorer and president of the Maritime Research Institute Mike Daniel, "Researchers are often drifting around without a rudder not sure what pirate stories are real, Then all of a sudden you find documents like these and it's like finding an island. There are solid facts beneath your feet." Daniel has been credited with discovering an unpublished reference to the Rose Emelye's capture in the Archives Départementales de Loire-Atlantique in 2008. Many of these discoveries help to shed light not only on Teach's career but his reputation as a fearless leader, menacing showman, and resourceful strategist.

Edward Teach was employed, like many other young men at the time, as a privateer stationed in the Caribbean during Queen Anne's war. Privateers, also called corsair or buccaneer, were civilian sailors who were given royal letters of marque for joining their countries' navies during wartime. As a privateer, Teach would have been in charge of commandeering enemy supply ships to thwart the war effort of opposing countries. He would also have the legal right to keep the spoils of any ship he and his crew overtook. After the war ended in 1713, many unemployed sailors like himself took to the sea and joined pirate crews in the Indian Ocean and the Caribbean. Some were in search of work and others were in search of rebellion.

CHAPTER 2: A PROFITEER'S RISE TO POWER AND PIRACY

I t is quite likely that after the War of Spanish Succession, Teach was one of the first groups of ex-privateers to end up in Nassau. He, along with 75 other men, followed a Jamaican privateer by the name of Benjamin Hornigold to the ravaged town in the summer months of 1713. Hornigold was already established in the area after being acknowledged by the governor of Bermuda and receiving mention in the American colonies' only newspaper at the time, The Boston News-Letter. Hornigold's gang would target small Spanish trade ships in the Florida Straits and isolated plantations in Cuba. In just eight months, they had accumulated a net worth of £13,175 which was considered a fortune at the time when a naval sailor might make £12 over the course of an entire year. Over the next few months, their wealth grew exponentially to £60,000. After running out the last of the authorities, pirates claimed Nassau for themselves and the population soared. Promises of riches and freedom drew people from every walk of life. Escaped slaves, smugglers, and prostitutes flowed into the area, as well.

One of the first historically accurate accounts of Blackbeard was recorded in December of 1716. He was now Hornigold's lieutenant and had control of a 90-man sloop. By the account, Henry Bostock described Teach as "a tall Spare Man with a very black beard which he wore very long." Blackbeard has been untruly depicted in many accounts as he was perceived by his enemies. A menacing and frightful figure with a long, wiry braided beard, the plaits adorned with black ribbon. In General History, he wore a sling made of silk across his chest with "three braces of pistols, hanging down in holsters like bandoliers." Dressed in all black from head to toe, he would also tie lit fuses under his hat to encircle himself in a halo of smoke and fire and give a truly supernatural appearance "more frightful" than "a fury from hell". General consensus has considered this show of intimidation as only just that. Merchant sailors would take one look at the wall of a man and his wild warriors with their crude weaponry and savage appearance and often surrender without firing a single shot. It was around this time that Teach's adversaries started referring to him as "Blackbeard".

Most examples of Blackbeard's leadership have actually shown a true sense of Democracy among him and his crew. The democratic process and social consciousness at work were obvious in regard to one story. After seizing a vessel, the pirates elected their captains by popular vote. They shared everything almost equally and most ships didn't accommodate a captain with his own cabin. Marcus Rediker, a maritime historian from the University of Pittsburgh commented, "They were very shrewd in the way they reorganized their ships to limit the captain's power." This ensured that crew members stood behind their captains out of respect and loyalty as opposed to duty or fear.

Despite his reputation, Blackbeard was reported to have been judicious with his followers and enemies alike. With the exception of his fatal encounter with the Royal Navy, there is not a single example of his use of lethal force among dozens of eyewitness accounts. A Trent University historian named Arne Bialuschewski claims he had not "seen one single piece of evidence that Blackbeard ever used violence against anyone." Bialuschewski is responsible for uncovering several accounts of captives and other

Jamaican archives in 2008. He claims that the monstrous image created of Blackbeard can be solely attributed to allied newspapers.

Of the swarms of pirates who sailed the seas during his time, Blackbeard was by far and large the most infamous. Unlike privateers, government-hired mercenaries tasked with attacking rival ships during wartime, Blackbeard and his crew were operating under their own flag. They were outlaws. Or at least that is how they were considered by the ruling class of the Spanish, British, and French colonies. Most of the population had a different view, however. These ordinary citizens elevated him to the level of a sort of Robin Hood and praised his rebellion against the crooked, oppressive, and tyrannical ruling class. As one of Teach's Bahamian associates put it, "They vilify us, the scoundrels do, when there is only this difference, they rob the poor under the cover of law...and we plunder the rich under the cover of our own courage."

These men and women were widely reputed as antiheroes; Regarded as so brave and noble that they have continued to pique our interest and captivate our imaginations through productions, novels, television shows, and pop-culture iconography. All of this material, including the works of Robert Louis Stevenson such as "Treasure Island", was largely inspired by either Blackbeard himself or the circle of pirates based out of the Bahamian islands for only a few short years from 1713 until around 1720. Despite their brief careers, the spirit of these notorious personalities such as Charles Vane, Stede Bonnet, Sam Bellamy, Jack Rackham, Mary Read, and Anne Bonny will continue to live on through the ages.

CHAPTER 3: ACCOUNTS OF REBELLION

Most merchant ships of the time carried little gold or "treasure", if any. They were usually responsible for cargo such as rum, grain, sugar, and molasses from the New World. As well as their cargo, the usual targets of most pirates would typically have other useful tools and supplies on board. Things like weapons, ammunition, and rope would be taken as spoils and divvied up between the crew in the event that the ship was overtaken. For the most part, the equal division was observed with the exception of captains and certain officers that received a larger portion. Some ships carrying passengers were targets as well, and at other times, the ship itself was the prize.

On one occasion, Blackbeard took control of a ship departing Charleston carrying wealthy passengers. He took them all as hostages, locked them in a hold of the ship, and threatened to execute them all unless the townspeople of Charleston delivered a ransom – a chest full of medical remedies. When the deadline for delivery passed, many hostages on board started to become uneasy. At the last moment, the citizens of Charleston came up with the ransom and the hostages were released, but not before having all of their jewelry stolen.

Blackbeard's first official solo command of a vessel came about by rather unusual circumstances. Some would consider it fate while others considered it merely happenstance. Towards the end of the summer of 1717, A strange vessel came limping into Nassau Harbor. Captained by an unlikely character, Stede Bonnet, a 29-year-old gentleman from Barbados. As a matter of fact, he came to be known as "The Gentleman Pirate". Largely due to his background as a wealthy landowner and heir to a sugar plantation. Citing marital problems by and large as the reason he resorted to a life of piracy, Bonnet had a ship built that he dubbed, Revenge. He and his paid crew traveled along the Eastern coast of what is now the United States capturing, plundering, and burning other vessels. While sailing toward the Pirates' Republic in Nassau, Bahamas, he lost a third of his crew and sustained major injuries during a confrontation with a Spanish warship. Bonnet and what remained of his crew sought refuge in the Bahamian harbor and with the support of many of the men, turned his ship over to Teach. Bonnet would stay confined to his cabin due to his injuries while Teach commanded his ship in some of the most daring piracy operations the colonists had ever known.

In the first few weeks of October 1717, Teach, now in command of Bonnet's ship, Revenge, terrorized the Chesapeake Bay as well as the New York and Philadelphia Harbors. He became the most feared pirate amongst the colonists, capturing 15 vessels and never staying in one place for long. Captains of the ships that encountered Blackbeard staggered into New York and Philadelphia with stories to tell. Tales of pirates cutting down their masts and their anchors; cargo thrown into the sea; entire slave ships taken, possibly due to the fact that they would rather join the ranks of the Caribbean pirates than suffer the fate that awaited them on shore. Philadelphian merchant, James Logan wrote to a friend in London after one of Blackbeard's raids, "Pirates...now Swarm in America and increase their numbers by almost every Vessel they take. If speedy care is not taken they will become formidable...and [they] know our govern[men]t can make no defense."

Long before any sort of military authority was

alerted, Teach and his crew was already on their way to their next conquest. The townspeople and local officials that inhabited the areas turned a blind eye to Blackbeard's presence and "import business" as the stolen goods he sold, like sugar and cloth, were much cheaper than those imported from England.

Toward the end of 1717 and into early 1718, Teach and Bonnet continued south to raid Spanish shipping ports in Mexico and Central America. The Spanish were well aware of Blackbeard's terror on shipping lanes off the coast of Veracruz and referred to him as "The Great Devil." By the spring of 1718, they had obtained close to 700 men manning several ships when they arrived back in Nassau to split the conquests.

In the fall of 1717, Blackbeard and his crew intercepted the French slaver named La Concorde near the Windward Islands. The ship was monstrous. At almost 250 tons, it was as big as the Royal Navy frigates that were stationed in the Americas and possessed enough gun ports to accommodate 40 cannons. However, the ship was no match for the pirates. The monstrous slaver was unable to outrun Blackbeard's smaller and more agile sloops and the majority of La Concorde's cannons were left in France in order to make room for slave cargo below deck. During the eight-month journey, sixteen of La Concorde's crewmen had died and a number of the survivors were suffering from illnesses like scurvy and the "bloody flux", according to the accounts of their officers which were found in 1998 by Mike Daniel. Captain Pierre Dosset surrendered the ship without a fight.

The ship was taken and refitted for piracy. The food and valuables were divvied up amongst Blackbeard's crew but what became of the human cargo? Pirate vessels were the exception in European America as a place where slaves could free themselves. A large number of pirates were of African descent and according to accounts, there were around 30 Africans in Bellamy's crew alone. In the months following the capture of the Concorde, witness reports claim that as many as 70 Africans were serving on Blackbeard's crew. Black sailors aboard pirate ships were not enslaved. They were free, independent contractors working under the captain of their choosing. There are accounts of groups of rebellious slaves rowing offshore to join pirate ships. The pirates could count on their commitment because the only other choice for them was a horrific fate of indentured servitude on the plantations in the area. Not everyone was so lucky, however. In the case of Dosset's slaves, only 61 of the 455 that were on board were taken as crew members. The others unfortunately were ferried back to auction in Martinique. The process of the decision on who was able-bodied enough to serve on Blackbeard's crew is a mystery but what is well-known is the fact that a substantial number of Africans would remain in Teach's inner circle until his death.

The Queen Anne's Revenge was now the center of Blackbeard's fleet. He and his crew continued to sail up the Lesser Antilles, a chain of islands dotting the outer rim of the Caribbean. By accounts of testimonies of his captives and letters from colonial officials, he set part of Guadeloupe Town ablaze and burned a flotilla of merchant's vessels near a British fort on St. Kitts. The governor of the Leeward Islands was forced to abandon a tour of his colony for fear that his vessel would be captured. Blackbeard also burned an English sloop in St. Croix exclusively for amusement then sailed for Puerto Rico. In early December, they learned of the captain of a merchant sloop that they had seized.

A decree was issued by King George I that stated any pirate who surrendered to the British government by September could keep his plunder and be pardoned for all crimes committed before January. Blackbeard's character was revealed by his next action. No records existed for the pirate for the next three months and were last seen sailing toward Cuba. Spanish merchants spoke of "The Great Devil" who stalked the Gulf in a treasure-filled ship. A newspaper out of London reported Blackbeard and Bonnet had been seen in winter around the port of Veracruz, hunting for a galley named the Royal Prince and the HMS Adventure which was the most powerful Royal Navy ship in the Western Hemisphere. Speculation is that Blackbeard had gone to lie low somewhere until he found a safe way to receive the king's pardon.

The rumors were, in fact, true. According to the papers of Captain Thomas Jacob of the HMS Diamond, who served as an escort for the Royal Prince, the handwritten papers include accounts from merchant captains about how Blackbeard had overtaken their ships in the Honduran Bay Islands by anchoring nearby and seizing officers after they rowed in. One witness who had spent nearly three months aboard the Queen Anne's Revenge claimed that they had sought to seize the Adventure. Another record stated that they "often threatened to take his majesty's ship the Diamond, as they heard she was weakly manned." Teach's intelligence was unmatched. These letters suggest that his warship's crew was significantly weakened by tropical diseases while they were en route to Veracruz. Blackbeard had been planning to risk everything in order to make one final massive score. Unfortunately for Blackbeard, he was never able to find the Royal Prince. He spent the majority of the spring in the islands surrounding Honduras and Belize seizing ships carrying wood and molasses, rather than gold and silver. His crew, despite capturing a large number of vessels, had very little to show for their efforts. Morale was low and for a time, they ran out of rum. "A damned confusion among us!" Blackbeard was reported to have entered his journal which was found by naval officers after his death. Citing the lack of plunder and rum, he headed off threats of mutiny.

The following spring, Blackbeard headed north. His fleet of four vessels took port in Nassau to sell goods and then tried to dive among the Spanish treasure fleet wreckage on the Florida coast. In May, he began the blockade of Charleston Harbor for six days capturing any vessel he could. Charleston's customs records for the weeks of the blockade were uncovered in British archives. Most of the cargo he took was generally useless. Mostly barrels of tar and rice. On discovery of the cargo, Blackbeard seized passengers for ransom, instead. They ended up leaving the area with a take of only £2,000. One of his prizes, however, was a chest full of medical supplies that were given as a ransom for hostages taken aboard a passenger ship. While excavating the wreckage of The Queen Anne's Revenge, researchers uncovered a pewter urethral syringe containing mercury, which was believed at the time to be a cure for syphilis.

Blackbeard spent quite a lot of time near Ocracoke Island. It became one of his favorite hide-outs, largely due to the fact that the coast of

North Carolina was flush with tidal inlets that offered cover and protection. Another reason that pirates were often attracted to this area, was the fact that the government had a less-than-strict policy concerning piracy, as was obvious during the relationship between Blackbeard and Charles Eden. He regularly turned a blind eye to activities occurring off his coast in exchange for a share in the spoils.

Following the grounding of the Queen Anne's Revenge at Beaufort Inlet, Blackbeard and the remainder of his crew headed for sanctuary in a small Spanish-built sloop. A day's sail from Beaufort off Pamlico Sound was the small frontier settlement of Bath. The small town, which was considered the capital of North Carolina, was only home to about 100 residents including Governor Charles Eden. Eden was considered a wealthy English nobleman placed in power over what was essentially an impoverished colony situated in the deltas and swamps of the North Carolina coast. The small number of residents spread themselves out amongst the low-lying cypress forests, murky creeks, and inlets. Comprised of only around 20,000 settlers. Most were poor and outnumbered by aggressive native tribes, who only a few years earlier, had all but wiped out the city of Bath and the rest of the colony. Blackbeard's men had come to collect on the King's pardon, including their activities during the blockade of Charleston Harbor. With their arrival, the population of the small town nearly doubled. It was also helpful that the newcomers were armed and seasoned combat veterans, as the townspeople needed all the help they could get concerning native tribes.

Blackbeard then went to see the Eden in order to accept the King's Pardon. In secret, however, the two made a deal. They realized that they could steal far more by working together. Charles Eden agreed to officially license Blackbeard's remaining vessel as a war prize and allowed him and his crew to sail back and forth from a nearby inlet attacking passing ships. One account claims that the crew took a French ship loaded with sugar and cocoa and then sailed it to North Carolina. Claiming they found it abandoned, this crooked partnership allowed them to divvy up the spoils and conduct business away from the public eye. On their arrival in Bath, Eden granted all of Teach's men a pardon and even the title to the sloop they had arrived in.

Teach and a number of his men decided to settle in Bath. They built homes and Blackbeard even married to a local girl by the name of Mary Ormond. Word of the pirate's "settlement" reached the ears of Royal Navy officials in Virginia who then sent dispatches to London about their activities. However it may have seemed,

Blackbeard and his men were totally content on using Bath as a new Nassau. They would sail down the creek and out into the open ocean preying upon any ships that passed down the Eastern Seaboard and the Chesapeake Bay. With the partnership of Eden and the tolerance of the general public, they thought that they had found a new Utopia. It was the perfect arrangement. Best of all, they assumed the sovereign government would not be subject to the British invasion.

That summer, Blackbeard grew even bolder. He took his small Spanish sloop out to the open sea.

On the morning of August 24th, they succeeded in capturing the Toison d'Or and the Rose Emelye, two French cargo ships. True to their modus operandi, Blackbeard's crew proceeded to use intimidation and terror to obtain their goal. The French sailors were all left unharmed. In an account by shipmate Pierre Boyer, one of the discoveries of Daniel in the archives of Nantes, they tied up a handful of crewmen while two armed men searched them all for valuables. The capture of the Rose Emelye proved to be a massive success. As well as the ship and a number of other supplies, hundreds of bags of sugar and cocoa were taken by Blackbeard and his men. The remaining crew were all transferred to the Toison d'Or and were ordered to "make without delay" to France or their ship would be burned. The closest reference to "walking the plank", as depicted by modern pirate accounts, occurred while crewmen were boarding and the pirates informed them that if they hadn't had a spare vessel, they would've been thrown into the sea.

The Rose Emelye was brought back to Ocracoke where her cargo was stored in tents on the beach. Blackbeard then set sail in a small sloop to deliver a bribe of sugar and chocolate to colonial authorities. That night he visited Tobias Knight, the customs collector and chief justice of North Carolina. The next day, Governor Eden granted Teach with salvage rights to the slaver, which was allegedly found abandoned at sea. The relationship between Teach, Eden, and Knight seemed to be a cushy deal. However, the governor of Virginia was less than pleased with the dealings of this group. Alexander Spotswood had been keeping an eye on Blackbeard for months via spies he dispatched into North Carolina in order "to make particular inquiry after the pirates." When he was informed of the corruption surrounding the Rose Emelye incident, Spotswood wrote, "I thought it necessary to put a stop to the further progress of the robberies." Unfortunately, Spotswood did not possess the authority to interfere with surrounding colonies, but he was not one to be tied down by pesky legalities. Actually, certain legislators had already brought to attention his squandering of tax revenue on Williamsburg's new Governor's Palace and a number of unethical power grabs. Spotswood had given himself around 85,000 acres of public land through blind trusts. The area had come to be known as Spotsylvania County. In an effort to quell Blackbeard's advances, he and the captains of two naval frigates in Hampton Roads developed a rather illegal plan to rid the coast of piracy.

CHAPTER 4:
THE DEATH OF
AN OUTLAW

Since the group was unsure as to the location of Blackbeard and his crew at the time, they launched a double-pronged attack on their southerly neighbors Bath and Ocracoke. Armed men on horseback arrived at Eden's home in Bath a week later. The other 60 men were dispatched in two small, unarmed sloops provided by Spotswood and captained by Lieutenant Robert Maynard. They arrived in Ocracoke, where Blackbeard's sloop was anchored, five days later.

In the darkness, both crews prepared for battle. The sounds of delegation and swearing floated across the water through the night air. The pirates, unlike their fearless leader, were preparing for the worst. They piled ammunition onto the deck, soaked blankets to put out fires, and spread sand over the deck to soak up spilled blood. One pirate even asked Blackbeard if his wife knew where he had a treasure hidden to which he replied that only he "and the devil knew where it was, and the longest liver shall take it."

When the sun rose the next morning, Lieutenant Maynard's men launched their attack. Blackbeard took the first point, outmaneuvering the unfamiliar crew and running them into a sandbar. Before the naval sailors freed their vessel, Blackbeard had prepared his own ship for battle and greeted them with a force that killed and injured a majority of the opposing crew. As the pirates fled for the open sea, a musket ball damaged a halyard in their sloop, resulting in a drop of one of their sails and a critical loss of speed. The second sloop of Lieutenant Maynard's had caught up to them but ended up receiving another broadside attack of grapeshot and hand grenades. A whopping number of 21 crew members were killed or wounded within a matter of mere seconds. Blackbeard prematurely considered the battle won and ordered his vessel alongside Maynard's so as to gain control of it. Blackbeard stepped onto the deck with rope in hand to tie the vessels together.

Blackbeard and his crew had been tricked. Lulled into a false sense of victory by Maynard and a dozen uninjured sailors. As soon as Teach and his crew set foot on the enemy ship, a surprise attack was launched by those lying in wait in a hold below deck. The pirates were taken aback. Suddenly engaged in hand-to-hand combat, Maynard and Blackbeard faced off in a battle that would later serve as inspiration to many pop culture references, movies, and books. His cutlass in one hand and a pistol in the other, Blackbeard stood to face his aggressor. They both fired their pistols but Maynard's hit its mark. Blackbeard had been shot. In a final move, he swung his cutlass wildly and hacked off Maynard's sword blade. The mighty pirate fell to his knees on the deck of the small sloop "with five shots in him, and 20 dismal cuts in several parts of his body." By Maynard's record, the second sloop then arrived to overwhelm the remaining crew. Maynard's crew then returned to Virginia with Blackbeard's severed head hung from the bow as a symbol of warning and victory, and with 14 prisoners, five blacks and nine whites.

The immense controversy surrounding the ambush served to finally bring justice to Spotswood in 1722. Eden, though he was cleared of all the charges brought against him, never recovered his reputation once his crooked dealings with Blackbeard became known and perished in the spring of 1722 due to yellow fever. The passage, "He brought the country into a flourishing condition, and died much lamented", appears etched onto his gravestone. Edward Teach's beheaded body was unceremoniously dumped into Pamlico Sound while his head was claimed as a trophy by Spotswood, who showcased it on top of a pole in Hampton Roads as a warning. The site was since dubbed Blackbeard's Point.

What legacy of the corrupt imperial elite such as Eden and Spotswood existed has since been buried under the larger-than-life and some would say noble accounts of Blackbeard and his associates. Popular culture, literature, and films have long been sensationalizing piracy and have, if even possible, made Blackbeard far more famous in death than he ever was in life. The lives these men and women led and the ideals they possessed will continue to live throughout history and on in days to come. Part of their success can be attributed to their use of a Democratic system and ability to govern themselves in business and in a deeper sense, united them in a common rebellion against the wealthy colonial elite. They became, in a way, heroic figures in the common republic. They were revered and respected for their courage. They set an idealistic example of enterprise, opportunity, and freedom.

Through the findings of emerging accounts

and from archives buried deep under piles of history, we have gained a better understanding of the true sense of grit and commitment these rebels possessed. They were considered true anti-establishment capitalists and adhered to their cause even after being offered multiple pardons and second chances. Most were hanged for their crimes or went down in a hail of gunfire and smoke like Blackbeard. While the world has seen a great advancement in the procurement of knowledge and more information is available on the subject than ever before, many questions still remain unanswered. Researchers continue to sift through the sands below the sea and through archives buried by time.

CHAPTER 5: THE QUEEN ANNE'S REVENGE

The vessel had been built in England in 1710 but was captured by the French a year later and renamed La Concorde de Nantes. She was modified by the French to hold more cargo and was being used as a slave ship. For Blackbeard, slavers made a perfect pirate ship. They were large, fast, and could be equipped with lots of armament. They could be easily converted to an open, flush deck which could house crew members and allow them to move freely. Blackbeard sailed the captured ship to a secluded area where they began outfitting it as a pirate frigate. Blackbeard claimed La Concorde as his flagship, renaming her Queen Anne's Revenge and adding a number of cannons. The name probably came from the War of Spanish Succession in which Teach had served as a profiteer in the Royal Navy. Blackbeard sailed from the west coast of Africa attacking Dutch,

Portuguese, and British merchant ships along his path back to the Caribbean.

After the blockade of Charleston harbor in May 1718, refusing the Governor's pardon, Teach ran aground the Queen Anne's Revenge in Beaufort Inlet. According to a deposition given by David Herriot, the former captain of Adventure, "Teach's ship Queen Anne's Revenge ran aground off the Bar of Topsail-Inlet." Teach then fled the ship after transferring supplies and crew onto a smaller sloop. Some of his crew members ended up stranded on a small island nearby and were later rescued by Stede Bonnet. Whether the grounding was intentional or accidental has been a matter of debate for scholars and researchers throughout the years. Some believe that he intentionally ran his ship ashore to weed out some undesirable crew members. Others, like maritime historian Daniel Moore, took clues from the wreckage of the Queen Anne's Revenge as proof that the event was unintentional. Afterward, Blackbeard did briefly surrender and accept the royal pardon which was offered to him and his crewmen by Charles Eden before going back to a life of piracy.

In November of 1996 the private research firm, Intersal Inc., discovered a wreck believed to have been Queen Anne's Revenge. She was located by Mike Daniel, Intersal's director of operations, who used research provided by maritime archaeologist David Moore. The ship lies in 28 feet of water about one mile offshore of Fort Macon State Park. Thirty-one cannons have been identified and more than 250,000 artifacts have been recovered. Swedish, English, and French cannons of different sizes were found on board. Their difference of origin is to be expected from a ship such as the Queen Anne's Revenge and other pirate ships of the time.

In November of 2006 and 2007, there was another round of artifacts discovered at the shipwreck and brought to the surface. These were considered confirmation to support claims of the wreck truly being the Queen Anne's Revenge, as there was a high level of doubt after the first discoveries. Additionally, in support of this theory, the cannons were found to be loaded and there were more of them than a ship that size would usually carry.

A third of the wreck had been fully excavated around the end of 2007. Part of the hull, including the keel and the mast, was left intact. The 1500 lb. sternpost was recovered in 2007, as well. Artifacts have undergone conservation with the North Carolina Department of Natural and Cultural Resources. Other artifacts uncovered during 2007 include cannon aprons, ballast stones, a sword gun, nesting weight, coins, and some loose ceramic fragments.

CHAPTER 6: THE GOLDEN AGE OF PIRACY

Throughout maritime history, certain times of piracy during the early modern period were marked as the Golden Age of Piracy. The most widely-accepted claim is that the Golden Age occurred in three separate outbursts in the years spanning from 1650 to the mid-1730s. These three can be broken down into three distinct bursts of activity and are commonly known as the buccaneering period, the pirate round, and the period after the Spanish Succession. The buccaneering period lasted from approximately 1650-1680. It can be characterized by the presence of English and French seamen attacking shipping routes in the Caribbean and finding refuge in Tortuga and Jamaica. The term "buccaneer" was derived from the term boucans since they were hunters originally. Living off the land on islands in the Caribbean. These men were rough around the edges, arming themselves with animal skins, knives, swords, and muskets. The buccaneers had a deep disdain for the Spanish after an altercation that forced them off their land. Those who fled to Tortuga became known as the Brethren of the Coast.

By the 1630s, some were employed as privateers and some were simply out for revenge on the Spanish. Their dress had evolved from the primal skins of the past to whatever articles of clothing they could plunder from their conquests. Weaponry evolved as well, introducing the hanger, flintlock pistol, and matchlock musket. The technique of these wild men was of much surprise to Spanish captains and other imperial elite. The buccaneers would disable and stealthily board their targets ship under the cover of darkness. Most were expert marksmen, and quickly eliminated the officers and helmsmen on deck. They developed a barbaric reputation, which was just as well. After a short time, crews would be instructed to surrender as a standard procedure during a raid.

Much that is presently known about this era is through the help of written accounts. Namely, that of Basil Ringrose, a surgeon that sailed with Bartholemew Sharp from 1680 to 1682 and kept a detailed journal of their travels along the coast of South America, as well as the book, The Buccaneers of America, by Alexandre Exquemelin. These men were largely in search of the riches of the Spanish. Gold and silver they piled aboard their convoys. During the time between 1530 and 1735, the fleet made an annual voyage to the Caribbean, which was dubbed the Spanish Main during the sixteenth century. Once they reached the warm water, they would then split up into three groups. One of which, sailed forward toward Porto Bello for the silver primarily mined in Peru, Columbian emeralds, gold from Ecuador, and Venezuelan pearls. Sailing another route, the second ship would have hoped to intercept trade routes in from Mexico where silk, silver, and spice were being shipped to Spain. The last landed in Honduras for the exotic spices and dyes of Central America. The pirates were nearly always successful, and with their prizes safely stowed aboard, they then headed for Cuba to gather and form one single convoy.

The ideals of the buccaneers, however, differed slightly from those who came after them. Stemming from what most believe was an extreme hatred of the Spaniards, a few of these men became infamous for the level of cruelty brought upon their enemies. Two of the most mentionable would include Brazilliano and L'Olonnais. L'Ollonais, previously known as

Jean David Nau, joined the buccaneers in 1962 and within only seven short years, proceeded to gain a fearsome reputation even among the battle-hardened buccaneers. Another name worth mentioning is that of Rock Braziliano. Of Dutch heritage, and whose true name is the subject of much speculation, became a true buccaneer when he made off with a ship whose captain he had quarreled with earlier that evening. One account claims he was captured and tortured after his acquisition of a Spanish treasure ship. During this time, Braziliano, or so he came to be known, escaped imprisonment from Campeche. He was also reported to have retaliated by spit-roasting two Spaniards alive because they refused to feed him. According to Exquemelin, "[he] would roam the town like a madman. The first person he came across, he would chop off his arm or leg, and anyone daring to intervene, for he was like a maniac." This attitude, reputation, and image of the buccaneers served them well. For, even though they were experienced and hardened, they were also smart. Why would you want to risk losing good men in a fight when you can intimidate your enemies and avoid altercation from the get-go?

One other mentionable mariner of the time was Sir Henry Morgan. Born in 1635, he was considered one of the better-known characters of the time. His show of competency and loyalty garnered him the honor of knighthood and the title of governor of Jamaica. Unfortunately, like most men, his career was short-lived at only ten years. He had gained fame by capturing ships and attacking cities. On his return to Jamaica, he became the owner of his first plantation. Seven years later, Henry Morgan was arrested and luckily kept in favor by the many connections he had made during his time in office.

Michel de Grammont, otherwise known as "Chevalier", once raided the town of Veracruz and held the 4,000 citizens he captured there for ransom. During the downslide of the age of the buccaneers, Grammont's ship became separated from the rest of his fleet during a storm off the coast of the Yucatan, forever lost to the sea never to be seen or heard from again.

The second wave of piracy occurred during what is referred to as the Pirate Round of the 1690s. This era is famous for its' incredible voyages from the colonies in search of East India Company targets in the Red Sea and Indian Ocean. These locations didn't experience the same volume of pirate activity as the coast of Africa and the West Indies. During most of the period, pirate targets remain the same. Imperialist ships from Spain and France. The Pirate Round was considered to have begun around the end of the 17th century when Thomas Tew was credited with coining the phrase in 1693. This was the beginning of the link between ports in the Indian Ocean and the Caribbean. Around the last decade, the pirates who followed Thomas Tew took advantage of this access and fled toward the Indian Ocean in search of fortune and fame.

In conjunction with Tew, who was eventually killed in battle during this altercation, a man named Henry Every captured the personally-owned ship of the emperor of the Mughal Empire of India, Aurangzeb. Including the insurance check, the entire haul has an estimated worth of £600,000. Through backward dealing within Parliament, The Emperor nominated William Kidd to rid the elite of their problems with Tew and his piracy. Kidd, however, after the death of Tew, turned to a life of piracy himself. He was considered responsible for the capture of the treasure ship Quedagh Merchant.

During the Pirate Round, another credible figure was a man by the name of Robert Culliford. An associate of Kidd, Culliford acquired the majority of his crew after the desertion of Kidd. After the 18th century, pirates such as Thomas Howard, John Bowen, Abraham Samuel, and Thomas White a second rise in profiteering saw the end of the Pirate Round.

The third and final branch of the Golden Age occurred during the time after the War of Spanish Succession from 1716 until 1726. This second wave of privateers, including Edward Teach, who were left unemployed after the war, turned to piracy along the West African coast of the Indian Ocean, and the eastern seaboard of North America.

CHAPTER 7: A WOMAN'S ROLE

When considering the history of women fighting for their respect, one specific story that comes to mind is that of Anne Bonny. She was renowned for her ruthlessness despite her gender. During her reign, Bonny and others like her challenged the notion that a woman's presence aboard a pirate ship would bring bad luck. A great majority of what is known of these women during the Golden Age is contained in a 1724 account which was discussed earlier entitled, A General History of the Robberies and Murders of the Most Notorious Pyrates. Bonny was born in Kinsale, Ireland around the year 1698. Her father, an attorney by the name of William Cormac, was engaged in an affair with his maid which resulted in him being left alone by his wife at the time. The maid, Mary Brennan, was left pregnant with Anne. William, in an unprecedented act, took his pregnant mistress and illegitimate daughter to South Carolina. To avoid any questions, Anne's father dressed her as a boy and claimed she was the child of a relative. Mary, Anne's mother, died in 1711, at which point, Anne was reported to have exhibited a "fierce and courageous temper." Records claim that she nearly beat to death a suitor when he tried to force himself upon her.

William, disapproving of his daughter's promiscuous and rebellious ways; disowned her in 1718 after scores of rumors about her had run his business aground and she married a poor sailor named James. The two sailed off in search of New Providence, now known as Nassau, Bahamas. Reports state that James then started a career as a bounty hunter for Governor Woodes Rogers, an ex-pirate, himself. Meanwhile, Anne spent her time in New Providence drinking and seducing other men. In A General History, Johnson states that she was "not altogether so reserved in the point of Chastity." Claiming that James Bonny had once "surprised her lying in a hammock with another man." After some time of this, Anne became enamored with a certain John "Calico Jack" Rackham. Anne soon left Bonny's crew to join the flamboyant Rackhams. Anne outwitted her opponents using not brawn, but brains. Reportedly, in what is considered the beginning of her pirating career, she fashioned a fake corpse by twisting the limbs of a mannequin and then covering it with fake blood in order to intimidate the passing French crew. The moment they witnessed her holding an axe over her bloody creation, they were quick to surrender their goods without alteration.

Surprisingly, a great number of women were drawn to the sea. Ranging from prostitutes, servants, and laundresses, to merchant sailors, and pirate captains. In all actuality, it could be said of Anne that she drew inspiration from a certain 16th-century Irish Woman by the name of Grace O'Malley. As such, she disparaged such rumors perpetuated by Blackbeard and others who strictly forbade women aboard their ships, believing that they were bad luck. Female pirates were often perceived as a liability and general anomaly. Mary, in disagreement with this sentiment, reportedly silenced a disagreeable shipmate by running a knife through his heart.

Anne, like other women who took on leadership roles during a male-dominated period of time, lived a double life. For personal affairs, she lived as a woman as Rackham's lover and helper. During the battle, however, she donned the attire of the other men: A loose tunic, a sword hitched by her side onto short trousers, a small cap placed atop her curls, and a holster thick with pillaged pistols. Often, the more exciting accounts of piracy are celebrated, but for the most part, the life of a pirate was fairly monotonous. Our associations of the profession are likened to the image portrayed by the imperial powers of the time. It's all propaganda and exaggeration. There is a variance concerning the accounts of when Anne met Mary Read. We know that Rackham had overtaken Mary's ship at an unknown location in the West Indies, and Mary was one of the many shipmates taken prisoner during the battle. Once all was said and done, Anne, who was dressed in feminine attire, attempted to seduce the newly acquired prisoner. Mary then informed Anne that she was, in fact, a woman. Reportedly even exposing her breasts to Anne as proof. A friendship, and depending on the source, a romantic relationship was formed at the time Anne had vowed to keep Mary's secret.

The two had quite a lot in common. Mary, also an illegitimate child, was dressed to resemble her deceased older brother. After her father died at sea, Mary's grandmother agreed to support her widowed daughter-in-law and her grandson, who unfortunately passed away. Mary's mother quickly became pregnant and then tried to masquerade Mary as her brother who her in-laws had so charitably agreed to care for since Mary's husband had died at sea. Once her family caught onto the rouse, they terminated their previous arrangement. After Mary and her mother were left to fend for themselves, Mary was often dressed as a boy and rented out as a house servant.

Mary, however, had become adept at living under the guise of masculinity. She served on a British ship as a "powder monkey" during the War of the Grand Alliance, shuffling bags full of gunpowder back and forth to the gun crews from the hold when she was only 13. After that, she was named a part of the Army of Flanders. She served both in the cavalry and the infantry. After falling for her bunkmate, she disclosed her secret to him. In the beginning, her love suggested that she become his mistress. It was written that "he thought of nothing but gratifying his Passions with very little Ceremony." But, Mary claimed herself a "reserved and proper lady". After this incident, she announced to her entire crew her femininity. She then left the army behind as well as the pirate to whom she confessed her true self to.

After her career in the army, she then resumed a masculine identity and set sail in a Dutch ship for the West Indies that was later captured by the British. Presuming that Mary was an Englishmen like themselves, the crew encouraged her to join their ranks. "Calico Jack" Rackham was serving as the quartermaster of this crew. Neither he nor his shipmates ever had any inclination of Mary's gender. She was ruthless. She was aggressive. She swore and drank on par with any other sailor. Always ready for a good raid, she was considered "very profligate", according to one of her many victims. Mary wore loose-fitting clothing that masked her feminine, "cursing and swearing much.", and sporting a clean face much like the majority of other mates on board who, in their late teens and early twenties, was also clean-shaven. According to multiple sources, Mary could have very well suffered from amenorrhea, an interruption or absence of the menstrual cycle due to malnutrition and stress.

In the beginning, Rackham was reportedly envious of the relationship between Mary and Anne. Believing Mary to be a man who was encroaching on his territory, Rackham had burst into her cabin, intent on slitting her throat. It was then that Mary opened her blouse and removed all misunderstanding. Mary's secret was safe from the rest of the crew. They proceeded to treat her as an equal, despite her gender. Mary and Anne fought together side by side during the battle. They dressed as men. Wearing jackets, trousers, and handkerchiefs tied around their heads, they would've fought with everything they had. Wielding pistols and machetes, they were "willing to do anything", one victim later claimed.

During the fall of 1720, Rackham and his crew took control of two small sloops and seven fishing vessels near Harbor Island. Mary and Anne then led a raid a few weeks later against a schooner, cursing and bullets flying wildly. They came into possession of tobacco, tackle, and pimento and held the crew captive for days afterward. This time of plenty would prove to be short-lived. On a dark night that October, the women noticed a strange sloop gliding silently alongside them. Once they recognized it as a governor's vessel, they sounded the alarm for the rest of the crew to join them on deck. As the result of a hard night of drinking, only a few regarded the call to arms. Jonathan Barnett, the captain of the governor's sloop ordered surrender, but Calico Jack had other plans. He took up his swivel gun and began firing on the opposing crew. A counterattack was ordered, and the exchange of fire began. Rackham's ship was eventually disabled due to gunfire and after seeing then that he was outnumbered, called for surrender and quarter.

The women, however, remained on deck and refusing surrender, faced the men alone. They swung their cutlasses wildly and fired round after round from their pistols. As legend has it, Mary was disgusted by the cowardice of her men that she stopped fighting to turn and yell into the hold, "If there's a man among ye, ye'll come up and fight like the man ye are to be!" When she was met with silence from beneath her, she proceeded to fire a shot into the hold which killed one of her men. Eventually, Anne, Mary, Rackham, and the rest of the crew were captured and taken prisoner. Captain "Calico Jack" Rackham was found guilty and sentenced to hang on November 18th. He made one final request, and that was for Anne Bonny.

She had one last piece of advice for him: "If you had fought like a man, you need not have been hanged like a dog." A week and a half later, she and Mary were put on trial in St. Jago de La Vega, Jamaica, at the Admiralty Court. Both pleaded not guilty, of course. One woman, Dorothy Thomas had testified against the two, claiming that the women robbed her in her canoe and that "the Reason of her knowing and believing them to be women then was by the largeness of their Breasts." Mary and Anne were sentenced to be hanged after a guilty verdict was revealed. Much to the surprise of court officials, the executions were halted due to the fact that miraculously, both women were found to be "quick with child."

Another infamous female pirate, Jeanne de Clisson, was a French woman who terrorized the public during the years 1346-1356. She had earned the nickname "the Lioness of Brittany" after her fearsome reputation was spread around. Her modus operandi was to mercilessly stab everyone aboard save one in order for them to go back and tell everyone that she was indeed responsible. Clisson lead a life of luxury up until the time that the French beheaded her husband for defecting during wartime. Vowing to avenge her husband's death, she sold off all of their possessions in order to purchase three of the largest warships her money could buy. She proceeded to have them all painted black and rose the crimson red sails. The

Black Fleet then began seeking out, robbing and destroying the King's Navy. Even after his death in 1350, Clisson continued to terrorize French shipping lanes. She would hunt down their vessels and find any noblemen aboard, she would swiftly hack off their heads with an axe and toss them into the sea.

The women who took up a career in piracy did so for many different reasons. Some, like Jacquotee Delahaye, were simply left with no other option. Descending from Haitian and French parents, Jaquotee was left in the care of her younger brother after the death of her mother and the murder of her father. In order to make ends meet for her family, she turned to a life of piracy. She faked her own death and lived as a man for many years to avoid persecution by law. Others, like Anne Bonny and Mary Read, were brought up in a world of deceit where their gender had been hidden from early childhood. Most of these women were strong-willed and highly independent warriors. They fought hard for their ideals, their families, and their equality.

CHAPTER 8:
THE LEGEND
LIVES ON

Edward Teach, or Blackbeard as he came to be known, can be considered the founding father of the pop culture pirate which is known today. However, though he and his associates have served as the inspiration for countless movies, productions, and books throughout the years, the stylized persona of Blackbeard and other pirates alike is very much an exaggeration of their true selves. While some pirates did commit brutal acts against their victims, most were surprisingly diplomatic and would have rather used intimidation and a fearsome reputation in order to conduct their business with little loss to their crew and ships. The action of "walking the plank" has been debunked as pure myth, as were hidden treasures of gold and jewels that were supposedly stashed by Blackbeard and other pirates. Many of these men and women were family-oriented. Captain Kidd, for example, was fiercely loyal to his children and wife in New York. According to Barry R. Burg, most sexual encounters took place not with prostitutes at the port, but with other shipmates. In this, most pop culture references thrive more on the exaggeration of fact than the fact itself.

Pirates often have a fearsome reputation of a criminal lifestyle, adventurous pursuits, and rogue personalities. They are quite often depicted as hardened, greedy, and cruel warriors, focused solely on fighting rival pirates in search of hidden gold and jewels. In popular cartoons, books, and even toys, they are portrayed in shabby clothing, with a handkerchief or a tricorne adorned with feathers. More often than not, they sport an eyepatch, flintlock pistols, cutlasses, and swords. Most modern depictions of pirates come equipped with battle wounds, scars, missing teeth (a common side effect of scurvy), wooden stumps and metal hooks where a limb previously existed, or exotic pets like monkeys or parrots. The stereotypical pirate accent is often that of South West England, and also Elizabethan-era English. Pirates in modern theatre and film possess an English accent and speech patterns that resemble a stylized West Country accent, as made popular during Robert Newton's Long John Silver in the 1950 Treasure Island. He also used the same accent in his rendition of Blackbeard the Pirate in 1952.

Historically, these men were more often than not ex-soldiers and former sailors who had renounced the idea of imperialism or fallen on hard times and turned to plunder the open sea for survival. Most accounts of pirates are that of a formerly respectable man who had fallen into squalor and piracy, resorting to a quest for buried treasure chests full of doubloons. In the mid-1990s, a parody holiday was created and celebrated on September 19th. International Talk Like a Pirate Day allows enthusiasts to release their "inner pirate", speak, and dress like the stereotypically portrayed buccaneers. International Talk Like a Pirate Day has gained popularity and momentum with the assistance of the internet since Venganza.org was set up with instructions on "pirate speak."

Captain Henry Morgan, who was discussed earlier, a Welsh privateer and admiral in the Royal Navy, made a name for himself by raiding Spanish settlements and is now immortalized as the namesake of Captain Morgan spiced rum. Davy Jones' Locker, as noted in the ever-popular Pirates of the Caribbean series, is another name for the bottom of the ocean. Sailors and ships who were lost at sea were said to have made a home in Davy

Jones' Locker. The true origins of this phrase are unclear, but a 19th-century dictionary connected Davy Jones to a "ghost of Jonah." The earliest recorded referencing of Davy Jones occurred in Four Years Voyages of Captain George Roberts, by Daniel Defoe, which was published in London in 1726. "They would look out some things, and give me along with me when I was going away; bug Roffel told them, they should now, for he would toss them all into Davy Jones's Locker if they did." Another mention of the phrase occurs in The Adventures of Peregrine Pickle by Tobias Smollett, published in 1751. Davy Jones, according to folklore, presides over the evil spirits of the deep sea and is often spotted perched among the rigging on the eve of a hurricane, on shipwrecks, and on other sea-faring disasters as a warning. Jones is described as a horned sea-beast possessing three rows of teeth, horns, and plumes of smoke trailing from his nostrils.

Concerning modern literature, the works of Robert Louis Stevenson would probably need to be mentioned first. Of his many works, the book Treasure Island served to personify pirates and create the elements such as how "X" marked the spot on a treasure map, and parrot-wielding, peg-legged seafarers. Originally, it was released as a series in Young Folks, a children's magazine from 1881-1882. It was renamed Treasure Island, or the mutiny of the Hispaniola. In November of 1883, the book was published under the pseudonym "Captain George North." A few true-to-life pirates were mentioned in the book such as William Kidd, Edward England, Blackbeard, Bartholomew Roberts, and Howell Davis.

Tim Powers' 1987 novel On Stranger Tides received nominations for the World Fantasy Award for Best Novel. It also took second place in the Locus poll for the best fantasy novel. The story is set during the Golden Age of Piracy and serves to feature true historical figures such as Stede Bonnet, Woodes Rogers, and Blackbeard. On Stranger Tides depicts Blackbeard in search of the Fountain of Youth. This story, in turn, served as inspiration for the fourth installation in the Pirates of the Caribbean films and a video game series by LucasArts named Monkey Island. Percy Jackson and the Olympians: The Sea of Monsters, a novel by Rick Riordan references Blackbeard, as well. The plot features Blackbeard and his crew who were all turned into guinea pigs and stranded on an island ruled by the dark sorceress, Circe. Percy and Annabeth manage to turn them back into humans at which point, they all escape on his ship the Queen Anne's Revenge.

The System of the World is another book that draws inspiration from the Golden Age. Written by Neal Stephenson, it is the third and final volume of The Baroque Cycle. It has been considered a genre-bender, boasting a historical as well as a satirical style. The work alludes to the third volume of Philosophia Naturalis Principia Mathematica by Issac Newton. Stephenson's book won the Locus Award for Best Science Fiction Novel as well as the Prometheus Award in 2005. It was also honored with a nomination for the Arthur C. Clarke Award in the same year.

Regarding television, Blackbeard has made appearances in a number of programs such as the Simpsons episode, "Treehouse of Horror IV" in which Blackbeard serves on the "Jury of the Damned.", in the 1968 serial Doctor Who, The Mind Robber, Blackbeard is summoned by the Master of the Land of Fiction during his mental battle with the Second Doctor. In a 2014 episode of Once Upon a Time, "Snow Drifts, "Fall", and "The Jolly Roger", Blackbeard was portrayed by Charles Mesure as the nemesis of Captain Hook. In the same year, Blackbeard was featured as the main character in the series Crossbones.

In 2014, Black Sails, the adventure-drama series was set in New Providence as a prequel to Robert Louis Stevenson's Treasure Island. Created by Robert Levine and Jonathan E. Steinberg for the Starz channel, Black Sails offered its free debut on YouTube and other streaming platforms in January 2014. Steinburg acted as executive producer alongside Michael Bay, Andrew Form, and Brad Fuller, while Levine and others served as co-executive producers. Black Sails experienced such popularity and demand, that in 2013, Starz approved a ten-episode second season that premiered in early 2015. The fact that the series was approved for a renewal before the first season even premiered, was largely due to the outstanding fan reaction to a showing at Comic-Con in San Diego. A third season was approved in 2014, and a fourth in 2015, all before the previous seasons had even released a premiere.

Black Sails is set during the Golden Age of Piracy, about twenty years prior to the events of Treasure Island. Captain Flint brings young crew members to fight for New Providence. During the first episode, in 1715's West Indies, the pirates threaten maritime trade agreements and the laws of imperial nations declared them enemies of all mankind or hostis humani generis. Historical pirates that are personified in the series include Benjamin Hornigold, Anne Bonny, "Calico Jack" Rackham, Blackbeard, and Charles Vane. During the first season, the series largely focuses on the hunt for a Spanish treasure ship the Urca de Lima. The treasure galleon ended up stranded during the beginning of the second season and guarded by Spanish soldiers. Toward the end of the season, however, Captain Rackham and his crew had stolen the treasure and carried it to the island of New Providence.

The inspiration of Blackbeard and other pirates of the Golden Age makes appearances in video games such as Sid Meier's Pirates! in which the Queen Anne's Revenge is captained by Henry Morgan. Blackbeard most notably stars in Assassin's Creed IV, Black Flag. The plot of the game features Blackbeard as an English captain who during the early 18th century, lurks around the West Indies and the eastern seaboard of the Americas aboard the Queen Anne's Revenge. In this game, the portrayal of Blackbeard is truest to account. Showing Blackbeard as a caricature of Teach and not at all the merciless outlaw that is commonly accepted. Blackbeard's fictional derivative is also embodied in the game Saints Row: Gat Out of Hell, and the game derived from the ever-popular Pirates of the Caribbean series, At World's End.

Through cinematic renditions of the Golden Age and otherwise, a personification of Blackbeard and his associates was created. The image of the modern pop-culture pirate can be largely attributed to the characters of films such as Blackbeard the Pirate of 1952 which was directed by Raul Walsh, The Boy and the Pirates of 1960 starring Mervyn Vye, and Blackbeard's Ghost of 1968 starring Peter Unistov and based on the novel by Ben Stahl. The most notable of these came in the year 2011 with the release of an adaptation of Powers' novel, On Stranger Tides. The production featured Ian McShane as Blackbeard. The film began as an adaptation at the time after Teach miraculously and fictitiously survived the Ocracoke Island battle with the assistance of his oracular quartermaster. This rendition of Blackbeard is again in search of the Fountain of Youth, is well-versed in the black arts, and wields a supernatural sword that allows him to bewitch his ship. In a description by Jack Sparrow, the fictitious protagonist famously portrayed by Johnny Depp, Blackbeard was "the pirate that all pirates fear." The film is set in a fictitious world ruled by versions of the East India Company, and the Spanish and British empires. Pirates in the series reflected the traditional notion in that they fought for freedom from imperial powers.

The entire saga began with the first release in 2003, Pirates of the Caribbean, The Curse of the Black Pearl, which grossed $654 million and received rave reviews from critics. After the success of the first film, the second film titled Dead Man's Chest was released in 2006. The sequel was so successful that it ended up as the number-one film of the year, grossing $1.1 billion. The third film, titled At World's End followed suit in 2007. Disney came out with a fourth, On Stranger Tides, in 2011 in 2-D, IMAX 3D, and digital 3-D. The final release also succeeded in raising over $1 billion and became the second film in the franchise, yet only the eighth in history to achieve such high profit. The entire franchise has grossed $3.73 billion worldwide and takes the prize as the eleventh highest-grossing film series in history.

A fifth installment, Dead Men Tell No Tales, is rumored to be released in the spring of 2017.

The latest fictitious cinematic portrayal of Blackbeard whom his first mate described as the "pirate of all pirates" was by Hugh Jackman in the 2015 Pan. Teach and his colleagues are the tyrannous rulers of the Utopian Neverland. He put out an order for his band of followers to kidnap the youth of Lamberth's boys' home in London to slave in the underground mines of NeverLand for a substance called Pixium, which is fabled to grant immortality.

CONCLUSION

I n conclusion, considering the constant discoveries of the present, more and more is being slowly revealed about the lives that these progressive men and women led. Over the course of history, The Golden Age of Piracy is quite possibly one of the most misunderstood periods of time. Thanks to the efforts of maritime historians like David Moore and others, we have more access now to the details of their lives than ever before. These accounts dug out of buried archives combined with the clues that were sifted out of the sands at the bottom of the sea offer a rare glimpse into the truth of pirates like Blackbeard and others of the time. The Golden Age was one of the most romanticized periods in history and spanned the course of centuries to see the rise and fall of empires bent on the colonization of the Americas. Often, pirates were branded by Imperial powers as enemies of the state and sentenced to death for their crimes. On the same token, the ruling class of Europe could also be considered enemies of humanity due to the genocide of entire native groups in the New World.

These men and women were considered one of the most progressive, anti-establishment groups of the entire era. They saw the rise of the slave trade as well as in shipping goods back and forth between new colonies. In contrast to the tyrannical rule of the time, pirates were uniquely democratic and are the earliest examples of freedom and liberty in such a time where these ideas didn't take hold in most places until centuries later. Piracy was far from a new concept. The practice has been observed throughout history wherever there were trade routes left unprotected. There are accounts as far back as the Roman and Greek empires and whether it was the Mediterranean trade or the Silk Road, there have long been pirates wherever there is unsuspecting and unguarded prey.

The widely-accepted personification of pirates is often a sensationalized caricature of the truth. Blackbeard and others like him, partially through their own intimidation factor and propaganda perpetuated by the imperial elite, carried fearsome and ruthless reputations. In fact, this was simply a method to ensure that they could overtake their target with little to no combat ensuring the safety of both their crews and ships. Men and women alike cultivated these reputations to place themselves on a sort of hierarchy. They had to be respected and feared by their crew and their enemies, alike. However, despite the image portrayed by popular culture, The Golden Age is so much more than just a few exploits of sea-faring outlaws. The pirates were responsible for committing robbery, murder, and destruction on a small scale compared to the actions of the powers that be, engaging in wholesale slavery and decimating entire Meso-American civilizations.

Considering this fact, it isn't that hard to decipher who the actual criminals were during that time. The royal elite of Spanish, English, French, and Portuguese are largely guilty of crimes far worse than all of the pirates of New Providence put together. The exploits of pirates during the Golden Age sparked a flame of rebellion that would echo through time to influence the Patriots during the American Revolution led to the expulsion of colonial powers from the New World during the 18th and 19th centuries.

Times of colonialism from the 15th through 19th century cannot be examined without considering privateers and pirates. They were, in a sense, the answer to Imperial colonization. Residing on the opposite end of the spectrum, these men and women banded together in rebellion and with a sense of brotherhood, they helped one another against the ruling classes of the time.

FREE BOOKS

Sign up for my newsletter for free Kindle books.

By joining my newsletter, you will be notified when my books are free on Amazon so you can download them and not have to pay!

You will also be notified when I release a new book and be able to buy it for a reduced price.

You will also get a free Spartans and the Battle of Thermopylae book delivered to your inbox (in PDF format) that can be read on your laptop, phone, or tablet.

Finally, you will receive free history articles delivered to your inbox once a week.

Simply click the link below to sign up and receive your free book:

https://mailchi.mp/2ebbbf6b6a7f/history-newsletter

Made in the USA
Las Vegas, NV
14 March 2024

87180407R00134